CALL

CHRIST

CW01085827

CALLED BY CHRIST

ANDREW MURRAY

CHRISTIAN ART
PUBLISHERS

Published in South Africa by CHRISTIAN ART PUBLISHERS
P O Box 1599, Vereeniging, 1930

© 2006
First edition 2006

Cover designed by Christian Art Publishers

Scripture quotations are taken from the Holy Bible, New
International Version®. Copyright © 1973, 1978, 1984 by the
International Bible Society. Used by permission of Zondervan
Publishing House. The "NIV" and "New International Version"
trademarks are registered in the United States Patent and trademark
office by International Bible Society.

Set in 12 on 15 pt Palatino by Christian Art Publishers

Printed in China

ISBN 1-86920-624-X

© All rights reserved. No part of this book may be reproduced in
any form without permission in writing from the publisher, except
in the case of brief quotations in critical articles or reviews.

06 07 08 09 10 11 12 14 15 16 – 10 9 8 7 6 5 4 3 2 1

Contents

About the Author

Andrew Murray (1828-1917) was an amazingly prolific Christian author. He lived and ministered as both a pastor and a writer in the towns and villages of South Africa. All of his publications were originally written in Dutch and then translated into English. As his popularity grew, Murray's books found their way into more than twelve foreign languages during his lifetime alone.

Andrew Murray's early writings were primarily written for the edification of the believer – building them up in faith, love, and prayer. They include *Humility*, *Absolute Surrender*, *Experiencing the Holy Spirit*, *Living to Please God* and *The Deeper Christian Life*.

Finally, in his last days, Murray addressed the issue of the Church and its lack of power on the earth. He emphasized the need for a constant and vital relationship with Jesus Christ and for consistent, fervent prayer.

Murray was an alert and intense man, continuing to write until his death at age eighty-nine. His burning desire to transpose all that lay on his heart and spirit to paper was revealed in the presence of several manuscripts in various stages of completion at the time of his death.

Andrew Murray has greatly blessed the Christian world with the richness of his spiritual wisdom and his ability to see and answer the needs of God's people.

CHAPTER 1

The State of the Home Church

> I am not ashamed of the gospel, because it is the power
> of God for the salvation of everyone who believes; first
> for the Jew, then for the Gentile.
>
> – Romans 1:16

I have a deep burden on my heart for foreign missions. But I have an even deeper concern about the one thing on which missions most depends: the state of the home church. Of course, by home church I mean any church that supports missionaries in foreign fields.

I vividly see the worldwide need of the gospel message. Furthermore, openings exist for bringing the gospel to every person throughout the world.

The piercing question is this: Will the church be able to enter these open doors? The state of the home church is an all-important factor in the possible solution of the great challenges in missions. Indeed, I have recently seen new meaning in the words *the state of the home church*.

Everything in foreign missions depends on the home base. Everything depends on the ability and readiness of the church to respond to God's call. It is well worth our while to read what some concerned pastors and missionaries have said about the life of the church:

As we contemplate the work to be done, we are conscious that the fundamental difficulty is not one of men or money, but of spiritual power. The Christian experience of the church is not deep, intense, and living enough to meet the world's need. We need a more perfect manifestation by the church of the spirit of the Incarnation and of the Cross. We need a new vitalizing of the whole church.

This renewal of the whole life of the church is indeed a great thing – an impossible thing, we are tempted to think. But does it seem so impossible when we get the conviction that God, being who He is, wills it? It does not seem so impossible when we saturate ourselves in the thought of the Gospels, with their repeated teaching, "Ask and you will receive" (John 16:24).

It is also worth our while to read the statements of other church leaders on this subject. The following section contains a summary of the thoughts on the state of the church.

Thoughts on Missions

The missionary problem of the church today is not primarily a financial problem. The problem is how to ensure a vitality equal to the expansion of the missionary program. The only hope of this is for Christians to obtain the more abundant life through Christ, which is given as we walk in the pathway of obedience to Him.

A crucial factor in the evangelization of the non-Christian world is the state of the church in countries that already have been evangelized. Until there is a more widespread consecration among the members of the home church, there can be no hope of expanding the missionary enterprise and making the knowledge of Jesus Christ readily accessible to every human being.

The most direct and effective way to promote the evangelization of the world is to influence Christian workers, and, indeed, the whole membership of the church, to yield themselves completely to the authority of Christ as Lord. We must establish and preserve at all costs those spiritual habits that will surely give us spiritual power and Christlike witnessing.

Above all else, we need to have such a spiritual atmosphere throughout the church that the very character and spirit of Jesus Christ will live anew in the hearts of all His followers, and that, through them, His life may flow forth to the world lying in darkness.

We are driven back, at every turn, to the question of the spiritual condition of the home church. Does the church have sufficient vitality for the tremendous task to which it is called? We realize that the fundamental problems lie in these areas: the sincerity of the spiritual experience of the church, the quality of its obedience, and the intensity and daring of its faith.

There can be no forward movement in missions, no great offering of life, without a deepening of the spiritual life of the church leaders and a real spiritual revival among the church members.

New methods can accomplish nothing unless they are begun, continued, and completed in prayer, and permeated from first to last with the Holy Spirit.

"Back to divine wisdom, back to the living power of Jesus Christ, back through prayer to the source of all power" – this must be the motto of all missionary organizations, all church leaders, and, ultimately, all church members. This is necessary if the Great Commission of our Lord Jesus Christ is to be carried out.

Therefore, we recommend that every endeavor be made to spread the spirit and habit of prayer among all Christian workers, young and old. We are confident that when the entire church will devoutly pray for the coming of the Kingdom, the triumph will already have been achieved.

We must make believers understand that it is only their halfhearted consecration and lack of faith that hinder the rapid advance of the work, only their own coldness that keeps back His redemption from a lost world. We must always bear in mind that He is eager and able to save the world, which has already been redeemed by Him. If only we, His professed followers on earth, were willing that He do so.

We frankly confess that it is futile to talk about making Christ known to the world unless there is a great increase of vitality in the members of the churches. It is the will of God that the most remote human soul have the opportunity to know Jesus Christ as his personal Redeemer. Of this there can be no doubt. We are all aware that the opportunity and means are sufficient. The work halts only because the entire church is not yet in full submission to His will.

Other church leaders see and speak in similar words of the same great need. Cooperation, if it is to lead to unity, requires a spiritual revival, which must be in its very nature supernatural. The reinforcements that are needed are dependent on the spiritual state of the churches that are to supply them. The very religions that Christianity is to replace teach her that her own life must first be lived on the supernatural plane, with the power of a living faith in a living God.

If our missionaries are to be fully and properly prepared to convince the world, they must go forth from a church in which the Spirit of Christ is evidently at work. They must go forth from a church in which the gospel is continually and irrefutably proved to be, in very truth, "the power of God for the salvation of everyone who believes" (Rom. 1:16).

Think on These Things

I urge you to consider these thoughts on the condition of the church. Think about them until you come to realize the intense seriousness of what that condition implies, the place that God calls the church to take, and what is needed if God and the world are to find the church ready for the work that awaits her.

Before us lies a world dying in its need of the very message that the church of Christ alone can bring. The world in its need is accessible and open to this message as it never has been in ages past. The Lord Jesus Christ, having laid down His life to redeem this world, still waits for the message of His redeeming love to be brought to those for whom He died. But His church does not have the power, vitality or consecration that would make it possible for her to fulfill her blessed task.

A revival is greatly needed. Something must happen if the plea for prayer for that revival is to be carefully obeyed by God's people. Something must happen if prayer is to be truly effective. That something is this: The state of the church as it has been described must become an unbearable burden. We must learn to give ourselves no rest, and to give God no rest, until He makes His church a joy on earth.

You are called ...

Our Savior waits for you to take the message of His redeeming love to those for whom He died.

CHAPTER 2

The Present Crisis

> Israel has sinned; they have violated my covenant,
> which I commanded them to keep. That is why the Is-
> raelites cannot stand against their enemies; they turn
> their backs and run because they have been made li-
> able to destruction. I will not be with you anymore
> unless you destroy whatever among you is devoted to
> destruction.
>
> – Joshua 7:11-12

An article once appeared in *The Missionary Record* that noted the serious decrease of membership in the church as well as the decrease in the number of young men offering themselves for the ministry. He said, in essence, "What sad proof this is of the lack of spiritual vitality in the church! What reason this gives for humiliation before God! What a call it is to the church to discover the cause of the evil and its remedy."

In the course of his remarks, he expressed a thought of the deepest meaning in these words: "Membership in the church implies that the only true measure of our surrender to Christ and His service is the measure of Christ's surrender for our salvation." In other words, we should surrender ourselves to Christ and His service to the same extent that He surrendered Himself for our salvation.

This is a very serious thought. Is it really true that the measure of Christ's devotion to God and to us in the sacrifice of the Cross is to be the measure of our devotion to Him and the service of His kingdom? It must be true. Yet how few Christians take time to think this through.

One almost feels that the minister who uses such an expression and has the vision of what it means could have no rest until he has lifted up his voice like a trumpet and called to the church, "Awake, you Christians, to your high calling – to have the same measure of devotion that Christ did in His surrender for you and your salvation."

Reflect on this thought until you realize something of its meaning; and then let your heart respond and say, "Nothing less, by the grace of God, will be the measure of my surrender to the person and the service of this beloved Redeemer."

If a thought like this could take full possession of even a small number of Christians, what power there would be in their witness to others of what Christianity really means! What hope there would be of rousing the church to find out and to confess the reason that the membership of the church and the number of theology students are so sadly decreasing.

The article closes with an appeal to all ministers and church members to renew their efforts on behalf of true godliness, and to work diligently so that young people may be brought to the knowledge of Christ and to a complete surrender to His service. Have they not already been doing this? There is no reason to doubt it. But what is needed is the discovery that the low spiritual life that prevails throughout the church is the true cause of the alarming decrease in membership.

"The measure of the surrender of Christ for us and our salvation, is the measure of our surrender to Him and to His service." If that is indeed to be regarded as the standard of church membership, how much more ought it to be the standard of the life and preaching of the minister!

God has put an incredibly important responsibility on the ministry. The whole tone of the church, the whole mind-set of the membership, depends on what rules the thoughts, heart and life of the minister. If the membership is to be lifted out of the worldly level, of which this decrease in the number of members is a sign, who is to do it if not the minister?

The God who has entrusted to ministers "the ministry of reconciliation" (2 Cor. 5:18) is the God who, by His Holy Spirit, worked in Christ the consecration that caused Him to give Himself as a living sacrifice. God will work a similar consecration in His servants when they fall before Him, confessing their weaknesses and sins.

Special prayer must be made for ministers, asking God to give them the vision of that great truth – that one standard of devotion to the salvation of men is required for both Christ and His ministers. If this vision comes to them, they, as the appointed leaders of the church, may be able to guide her in the way of repentance and restoration.

There is indeed a present crisis. In more than one church denomination, the same alarming disease has appeared. There is, indeed, a crisis throughout Christendom. Many leaders feel strongly that the church in its present state is utterly unfit and unprepared for the great work that God has put before her and expects her to undertake. Just read the following comments.

Professor Cairns asked, "Does the church have within itself at this moment the spiritual resources for so high and arduous a calling?" His profound conviction is that it does not. He said it is moving up to a situation that is too hard for it and for which it is not yet ready.

And so, the matter of most urgent concern before the church, which dwarfs all others, is how it can obtain from the eternal God those spiritual reinforcements of His grace that will enable it to meet the coming hour.

Dr. Denney said:

I speak only of the church to which I myself belong, but something similar, I believe, is true of almost every church in Christendom ... The number of candidates for the ministry at the present time is less than it was a good many years ago. It is hardly a sufficient number to keep up the staff at home, to say nothing of supplying workers abroad.

People are not coming forward as ministers, not coming forward as missionaries, because they are not coming forward into the membership of the Christian church at all.

Something must happen to the church at home if it is going to even look at the work that has been put upon it [in foreign missions].

The solemn words of Dr. John Mott, a pioneer

in the Young Men's Christian Association, are as follows: "I boldly say that the church has not yet seriously set itself to bring the living Christ to all living men!"

These statements are simply appalling. Imagine the church of Christ not being able to hold its own – actually defeated and driven back by the Enemy! Rich in the promise of the Father, it is nevertheless, in spite of its perfection of organization, unable to gather in souls.

Do we not have good reason to say, as Joshua did when he fell on his face before the ark of the Lord, "O Lord, what can I say, now that Israel has been routed by its enemies?" (Josh. 7:8).

The story of Joshua gives us the key to the question as to what is to be done to remove this terrible reproach on the church of Christ. God's answer was:

> Israel has sinned ... That is why the Israelites cannot stand against their enemies ... I will not be with you anymore unless you destroy whatever among you is devoted to destruction.
>
> Go, consecrate the people. Tell them, "Consecrate yourselves in preparation for tomorrow; for this is what the LORD, the God of Israel, says: ... O Israel. You cannot stand against your enemies until you remove it." (Josh. 7:11-13)

Something must happen to the home churches. What can it be but that God's people must fall on their faces before the Lord to confess their defeat with shame and humiliation? We must discover what it is that prevents God from giving that power and blessing with the Word that would give us the victory over the world.

Individually and collectively, we must put away the accursed thing that makes it impossible for God to reveal His presence in power in the church as He longs to do.

"Go, consecrate the people. Tell them, 'Consecrate yourselves in preparation for tomorrow.'" Israel was reminded that God is the Holy One and that sin is the only thing that can rob us of His presence. Israel was a holy people with whom holiness was the one secret of power and of blessing.

Joshua had used the same words when the children of Israel were about to cross the Jordan River: "Consecrate yourselves" (Josh. 3:5). At the Jordan River, God had shown His great power in bringing the Israelites through on dry ground. In this instance where Israel was defeated by her enemies, God would again reveal His divine power. This time it would be in teaching them to discover and to cast out the sin that had been the cause of defeat.

The same thing must happen to the church

today if it is indeed to listen to the call for the army of God to move on to the great world conquest.

The more we study these words from church leaders, the deeper our conviction will be that nothing less is needed than that we take our place with Joshua and the elders on our faces before God. There He will reveal the state of the church in such a way that will bring us to the end of all our hopes and plans.

There we will be brought, in utter weakness and in humble, persistent prayer, to urgently appeal to Him. We will entreat Him to give ministers and church members a revelation of sin on the one hand, but on the other, an understanding of the all-sufficiency of His grace to cleanse us and to make us holy. Such a revelation will induce us to give Christ His place as our leader on the path of victory.

Nothing will teach a backsliding church that comes to repentance what the love of Christ is more than the exercise of His power in cleansing and delivering from sin. It is the experience of what He can do for us that will rouse in us true loyalty to follow Him as He leads us in the path of victory.

CHAPTER 3

The Unsolved Problem

He died for all, that those who live should no longer live for themselves but for Him who died for them and was raised again.

— 2 Corinthians 5:15

The chief and most difficult problem of missionary work has not yet been solved. As I wrote in the last chapter, the most important problem of all is how the church is to be roused to a deeper and fuller life in Christ. Without this, there is no possibility of Christ being made known to all the world. Yet, our church leaders have not shown us how to begin and what to do.

In Dr. John Mott's book, *The Decisive Hour of Christian Missions*, he devotes the first three chapters to a survey of the mission field. He points out the hopeful signs, as well as the threatening dangers that urge immediate action.

Chapter four of his book bears the title, "The First Great Requirement: An Adequate Plan." After pointing out the almost insurmountable difficulties that must be overcome before the thought and life of whole nations can be changed, he asks, "How is such a seemingly impossible task to be accomplished?" He answers that the first essential is for the church to have a plan to meet the situation – a plan adequate in scope, thoroughness, strategy, and methods. His chapter is devoted to pointing out the main features of such a course of action.

If the church's task in the mission field is so difficult that it cannot be undertaken without the development of an adequate plan, what are we to think of the far harder task to which the church at home is called? How are we to rouse Christians out of their apathy and train them to become devoted servants of Christ, full of enthusiasm for the King and His kingdom?

In a previous chapter, we saw how strongly, almost hopelessly, various church leaders regard the state of the church. They have stated the problem with terrible clearness, but they have left it unsolved. They have not given us any plan for bringing about a change, and as yet there is not much indication that the churches are preparing themselves for this work of supreme importance.

Leading Christians to that deeper and more intense vitality, that more abundant life in Christ, without which the work cannot possibly be done, is a question of life or death.

It is with humble reluctance that I venture to make some suggestions as to what is needed if the churches are really to prepare themselves for the tasks ahead.

First of all, we will have to set clearly before ourselves and others the true calling of the church and of every believer. Christ expects everyone who knows His love to tell others about it. Christ requires everyone who is made a partaker of His redemption to yield himself, as the first purpose of his existence, to live for the coming of His kingdom.

Christ asks that, just as the loyal subjects of a king are ready in time of war to give their lives for the kingdom, so His redeemed ones, in the power of His Spirit and His love, will not live for themselves but entirely for Him who died and lives for them (2 Cor. 5:15).

As long as this calling is considered too difficult to fulfill and is not accepted as the very groundwork of the relationship between Christ and every member of His church, our attempt to lift the church into the abundant life will be in vain.

Unless God's children can be brought to accept this standard, to consider it their highest happiness, and to believe in the power of Christ to work and maintain it in them, there will be little hope of their obtaining intense vitality, without which the church cannot fulfill its calling.

The second step is to discover the real cause of the evil, its terrible power over us, and our utter inability to overcome it. It will not be enough to confess that we have been unfaithful to Christ's charge, that it is our fault that people are perishing in darkness. We must go deeper than this.

We must ask how it can be that, with our faith in Christ, there has been so little love for Him and the souls He has entrusted to us. How can it be that we could imagine that our activities were pleasing to God, while all the time we were grieving our Lord by neglecting His last and most cherished commands?

We will find that at the root of it all lies the selfishness that sought and looked to Christ for our own personal salvation; the worldliness that kept us from living in the power of His death and resurrection; and the self-satisfaction that rested content with a religion that operated, for the most part, in the power of human wisdom and only had the "form of godliness" (2 Tim. 3:5).

We will have to be brought to the conviction that we need an entire revolution in our inner lives. The God on whom we counted to bring us out of Egypt, in conversion and pardon, must bring us, by a still more mighty experience of His grace, into that life of the new covenant in which God will dwell with us and walk with us.

Who is to take the initiative in all this? Should it be a missions conference, which, with regard to the foreign field, seeks to formulate and master all that is needed in connection with the spiritual work?

Or, can we count on each church to consider the question separately and to give time in its assembly or council or congress to deal with this subject as one of the most important that could be brought before it? Should each church lead the way in the deep humiliation and fervent supplication that are absolutely essential if the longed-for change is to come?

Or, should it be left to individuals to gather around themselves small groups to begin the work of confession and intercession for the power of the Holy Spirit, through whom alone the supernatural renewal can be accomplished?

Also, who are to be the agents who will carry out this work? We all naturally think of ministers as God's messengers, who have been given by Christ to perfect the saints for their work of the ministry in building up the body of Christ (Eph. 4:12). But ministers need prayer. Paul felt how absolutely dependent he was on the prayers of believers. Let us begin at once and implore God to raise up ministers who have the courage of their convictions, who will sound the call to a new repentance and a new consecration. May they, in bold faith, declare what Christ is going to do for the church if she will only yield to Him.

We will need to look to the ministers, but we will also need to encourage every Christian who is earnestly seeking to serve Christ to take part in the great crusade for winning soldiers for the Lord's army. Many are longing for someone to lead them into a life of liberty and devotion to Christ, which they have seen from far away but have never yet been able to attain.

Let men and women take courage and speak out, telling those around them what happiness there is in a life spent for Christ and what unfailing strength can be found in Him.

Those who have already taken part in the great work of intercession for missions should begin to pray persistently for the renewal of the church around them. In this way, some hearts that have, so far, been content with the hope of heaven as the one aim of their Christian life, will begin to wake up to the attraction of Christ's claim, as it is brought to them by living witnesses around them. And God will certainly hear our prayers and give His blessing.

God is able to awaken carnal Christians. Observe what happened in the book of Ezekiel:

> Come from the four winds, O breath, and breathe upon these slain, that they may live. So I prophesied as he commanded me, and breath entered them; they came to life and stood up on their feet – a vast army. (Ezek. 37:9-10)

In this undertaking, everything depends on the supernatural, on the all-sufficiency of God, on His infinite love and power. He yields Himself to be led by the prayers of His children to the place where His Spirit is to descend, and to the work that He is to do.

Nothing less is needed than a new creation, a resurrection from the dead, which brings forth out of carnal, worldly Christians the new person in Christ Jesus, in which old things are passed away and all things are become new (2 Cor. 5:17). Nothing less than this is to be our aim and expectation. And the more absolutely we believe that God alone can and will revive the dead, the more simple and unceasing will be our persistent prayer that God Himself will do for us what to human thought appears impossible.

One more word. Let us never forget that everything begins with and depends on the individual. Let no one who hears the call of God to this new consecration wait for the church to act or wait for his fellow believers to act. Let him offer himself with his whole being so that Christ may be magnified through him.

Begin at once, and give God no rest until Christ has the place in your heart that He claims. Let devoted loyalty to His kingdom be the fruit of intense attachment to His person. Let His love become a holy passion, and let Him find in you one upon whom He can count to seek, above everything and at any sacrifice, to make His name known to every individual.

You can be sure that God will use you to lift others around you into the fullness and the fruitfulness of the abundant life in Christ Jesus.

God grant that the unsolved problem may find its solution in the fervent prayer of His believing people!

You are called ...
To become passionate about Christ's love
and make it known to every person.

CHAPTER 4

"Peace, Peace, When There Is No Peace"

They dress the wound of my people as though it were not serious. "Peace, peace," they say, when there is no peace. Are they ashamed of their loathsome conduct?
— Jeremiah 6:14-15

Over the last few decades there has continually come from one church or another the news of a decline in membership. This has become so widespread that reportedly today there is hardly a church that is not suffering from the same problem.

I am surprised that no church has earnestly determined to examine the cause. I wonder why none of the church leaders have sounded the alarm and called on the whole church to cry to God for the discovery of the root of the evil and the secret of its removal. In the spirit of the deepest humility and love, I express the fear that the prophet's words are too applicable: "They dress the wound of my people as though it were not serious. 'Peace, peace,' they say, when there is no peace" (Jer. 6:14).

Two years ago, the president of a well-known denomination made several comments about the state of the church. "To me it is questionable if many churches are doing much more than marking time," he said.

In other words, most churches are producing nothing, making no progress. "The atmosphere is impregnated with influences unfavorable to religious life," he added. But was that not much more the case in Corinth and Rome? Yet, the power of the Holy Spirit brought the very atmosphere of heaven, the power of the resurrection life, into those churches.

After mentioning many of the elements unfavorable to religious life, this Christian leader concluded, "Meanwhile, in my judgment, we have not yet touched bottom." Only when we have touched bottom can we go no lower.

In another article on this problem, the writer said, "The figures are unquestionably disappointing, though there is no reason for serious depression." Could it be that "serious depression" is just what God wants, and what is essential if we are to be fully convicted and see the evil as God sees it? The writer explained that:

There is an increase in the number of churches, and there is a marked increase in the number of Sunday school teachers. But the students are fewer by nearly seven thousand. Considering the greatly increased activity, the result falls far short of our hopes.

Does this not suggest the thought that building churches and increasing the number of Sunday school teachers is what man can do, while, in order to increase members and Sunday school students, we need a spiritual vitality in the ministers and teachers that none but the Holy Spirit can give?

Yet, it is alarming that people in our churches are afraid of nothing as much as "serious depression." Men say that "in business or finance there are also times of depression, but they do not always last. A change comes, and business prospers again. We must keep up our courage and hope on."

However, are we not in danger of forgetting one thing? When the depression has to do with business and money, every man concerned is ready, with his whole heart, to do anything he can to bring about the change. But, tragically, this is just what is not the case in the church. How few there are who, with their whole hearts, yield themselves to the power of the spiritual life and do their utmost to win to Christ the souls that are drifting away from Him and His church.

The article mentions that only about one fifth of Sunday school students ultimately connect themselves with the church. What a thought: millions of students are entrusted to the church for three or four years of their lives, and yet the church is powerless to influence them to become its members!

If there is one problem that is worthy of the highest concern among our church leaders and needs the deepest waiting on God for the enlightenment and courage of His Holy Spirit, it is this extremely serious one. How are these millions of young people, whom the church is now unable to influence, to be reached and won?

The solution lies with God and with the believers who are willing to honestly face the situation. I am speaking of Christians who know what it is to have access to God and to receive from Him the teaching and power of the Spirit.

The chief suggestion that is given in the article in regard to the whole difficulty is contained in one word – work.

There have been too many conferences and meetings to discuss work — it is better to do the work. The minister is to be pitied who does not know what he ought to do in his sphere of labor. He is most deeply to be pitied if he does not know the source of true strength.

Yet, this last part is just the crucial question. Judging by what is being written and spoken, it is the lack of much intense prayer and living faith that is the cause of all evil. God's promise is sure. But the lack of conversions, the decline in membership, the decrease in Sunday school students, all indicate that the power of God is little known. Nothing can be more dangerous than to tell people to work if their method of work is not what it should be.

If I meet a weary traveler who is on the wrong road and try to encourage him by telling him that he must go bravely forward, that he still will be able to go a long way before evening, I am deceiving him. I ought to tell him he is on the wrong road and show him where to find the right one.

The article says, "Considering the greatly increased activity in various organizations, the result falls far short of our hopes." The activity may be two or three times as great, but if the worker has not learned to desire above all else the supernatural resources of God, which are given as the result of prayer for the power of the Spirit, all his work will be in vain.

No leader could do a greater kindness to the church than to help all her ministers gain a full understanding of the presence and power of the Spirit. When our ascended Lord spoke the words, "You will be My witnesses ... to the ends of the earth" (Acts 1:8), and, "Stay ... until you have been clothed with power from on high" (Luke 24:49), He gave a law for all time to His servants in regard to the secret of work. Daily receiving the Spirit through fellowship with God is the only secret of successful work.

People sent letters in reply to the article, and more than one suggested that there are other causes than those that had been named! One mentioned:

The lack of intimate Christian fellowship within the churches, which enables them to offer only a very small inducement to earnest souls. This defect grows out of the lack of spiritual life, the prevalent neglect of Holy Scripture and exposition.

Another said that:

In preaching, a personal appeal to the conscience and a direct effort for conversion are seldom wit-

nessed. This is largely a result of the same cause
[the lack of spiritual life].

A third stated the following:

In many of our churches the great underlying doctrines and facts of the gospel are scarcely ever referred to in preaching.

The question cannot be answered by simply
saying that every minister knows what he ought
to do. How many there are who have been doing
what they could and yet have failed.

Let us not think of it as demeaning the church
when we invite our fellow believers to test their
work according to the standards of the Word of
God. When a doctor tells a man that his wife is
suffering from a dangerous disease, he does not
demean the man's wife; he is doing the greatest
kindness as the first step toward healing.

Many years ago, Charles Spurgeon spoke
boldly about the decline. He was only warning
against what has actually come to pass. There
are thousands of hearts that feel deeply that the
church of Christ is in dire straits. Let us beware of
every thing like healing "the wound ... as though
it were not serious," or saying, "Peace, peace;
when there is no peace" (Jer. 6:14).

Let us rather listen to the word, "Let my eyes

overflow with tears ... for my virgin daughter – my people – has suffered a grievous wound" (Jer. 14:17). In listening to that word from God, we will find healing.

You are called ...

You will receive power when the Holy Spirit comes on you; and you will be My witnesses in Jerusalem, and in all Judea and Samaria, and to the ends of the earth.
– Acts 1:8

CHAPTER 5

*Why Could We
Not Drive It Out?*

---

*Then the disciples came to Jesus in private and asked,
"Why couldn't we drive it out?" He replied, "Because
you have so little faith. I tell you the truth, if you have
faith as small as a mustard seed ... nothing will be
impossible for you."*

— Matthew 17:19-20

When we read the story of the demon-possessed child in Matthew 17:14-21, we see
that the disciples felt ashamed that they were
not able to drive out the evil spirit. Before, when
Christ had sent them out to do the work, they
had come back rejoicing that the evil spirits were

subject to them. But here, in the presence of the Pharisees, they had been brought to confusion by their powerlessness. They felt it deeply, and they asked the Master to tell them what the cause of failure was. He answered, "You have so little faith" (Matt. 17:20). They had not been living in communion with God and separation from the world; they had neglected prayer and fasting.

When the church begins to see that the shameful decline in membership is because of the loss of a power that she had in times past and when she confesses that it is beyond her reach to find the cause and the cure, then she will learn to bow in penitent prayer for the Master to reveal to her the depth of the trouble and the only way out of it.

In this chapter, I will mention three men and their thoughts on this state of affairs. The first is the evangelist D. L. Moody. In an issue of the *Christian*, there appeared a letter from Mr. Moody to the *New York Independent* on the subject. He referred to a statement in a previous issue of that paper that "there are over three thousand churches [in certain denominations] in the United States that did not report a single member added by profession of faith during the year." Mr. Moody then asked:

Can this be true? The thought has taken such hold of me that I cannot get it out of my mind. It is enough almost to send a shiver of horror through the soul of every true Christian. Are we all going to sit still and let this thing continue? Should we not lift up our voice like a trumpet about this matter? What must the Son of God think of such a result of our labor as this?

In answer to Mr. Moody, the *Independent* explained that some allowance must be made for the new churches founded within the year, for small churches without a pastor, and for others that failed to send any report. The editor expressed his disagreement with what Mr. Moody had said in his letter about modern biblical criticism and other causes of the evil. And then he proceeded:

But, while all this is true, Mr. Moody does well to be astonished and pained at the thousands of churches that reported not a single member added by profession of faith last year. It is enough to send a shiver of pain through the soul of every true Christian.

Let us pause before we read on and ask, "What should all this mean to the church?"

The second man I want to mention is Dr. Forsyth, an English Congregational theologian. In his book, *The Cruciality of the Cross,* he wrote the following:

It is reported from most quarters in England that there is a serious decline in church membership. For this, several explanations are given. But it is well to face the situation, and to avoid excuses, and if we do, we may discover that the real cause is the decay, not in religious interests or sympathies, but in personal religion of a positive and experienced kind, and often in the pulpit.

Religious sympathies or energies are not the same as Christian faith. We have become familiar with the statement that there is as much good Christianity outside the churches as in. This is not quite false, but it is much more false than true. It would be true enough if Christianity meant decent living, nice ways, precious kindness, business honor, ardent philanthropy, and public righteousness.

But all these fine and worthy things are quite compatible with the absence of personal communion with God, personal faith as Christ claims it, in the sense of a personal relationship with Jesus Christ, personal repentance, and personal peace in Christ as our eternal life. Yet that is God's first charge to us, if Christianity is true. And it is this kind of Christianity that alone builds a church and its membership. Decay of membership in the church is due to a decay of membership in Christ.

Even among those who remain in active membership in our churches, the type of religion has changed, the sense of sin can hardly be appealed to by preachers now; and to preach grace is in many (even orthodox) quarters regarded as theological obsession and the wrong language for the hour, while justification by faith is practically obsolete.

The grace of God cannot return to our preaching, or to our faith, until we recover what is almost completely gone from our general, familiar, and current religion, the thing that liberalism has quite lost – I mean a due sense of the holiness of God. This holiness of God is the real foundation – it is certainly the ruling interest of the Christian religion.

Have our churches lost that seal? Are we producing reform, social or theological, faster than we are producing faith? We are not seeking first the kingdom of God and His holiness, but only carrying on with very expensive and noisy machinery a "kingdom-of-God's industry." We are merely running the kingdom, and running it without the Cross. We have the old trademark, but what does that matter in "a dry and weary land, where there is no water" (Ps. 63:1) if the artesian well on our premises is growing dry?

Let us take to heart the lesson: It is the lack of positive personal religion, sometimes even in the pulpit, that explains the decline in membership.

The Reverend F. B. Meyer, an associate evangelist of D. L. Moody is the third man whose thoughts on this matter bear relevance here. In an address on Acts 19 and the anointing power of the Holy Spirit, he said:

> There are four different planes of power – the lowest is the physical, above that is the mental, above that is the moral, and above all is the spiritual. It is only when a man moves on the spiritual level that he has power with God and has power over unclean spirits.
>
> It is because too many ministers and too many Christian workers today are content to live upon the intellectual level, or upon the moral plane, that their work is powerless to touch the mighty stronghold of Satan.
>
> The first question, therefore, to put to every Christian worker is, "On what level are you working; on what level are you living?" For if you are speaking on anything less than the Spirit level, know that your life will be largely a failure.

He then told the story of the seven sons of Sceva. They had tried to cast out an evil spirit in the name of "Jesus whom Paul preaches" (Acts 19:13). The evil spirit answered, "Jesus I know, and I know about Paul; but who are you?" (v. 15).

And the man with the evil spirit overpowered them and gave them such a beating that they fled, naked and wounded.

F. B. Meyer then said:

We have been praying that God would send converts to the churches and stop this awful ebb. Still the people are leaving our churches, and the pews are empty. We have no additions, or few, to our churches; and, pray as we may, we cannot avert it. Why? Why? Because the devil does not fear us. We have no power. The devil masters the church and masters the world, and here we are all powerless, and he says, "Jesus I know, and I know about Paul; but who are you?"

You remember the words of our Lord: "How can one enter a strong man's house ... unless he first ties up the strong man?" (Matt. 12:29). We cannot plunder the house, because we have not tied up the strong man. We have not tied up the strong man in our own house. We do not know what it is to master the power of evil in our own hearts. How then can we rescue the men who are led captive at Satan's will? It seems to me we have got to get back to prayer. O God, forgive us for our prayerlessness! God knows what a prayerless people we are. I do not wonder at things being as they are.

Let us learn the lesson. The decline in membership is nothing more than what can be expected where the work is not done in the power of the Spirit and in prayer. The spirit of darkness that rules in the world, which, with its mighty attraction, draws men from Christ and His church, is too strong for us. Nothing and no one can give the victory except the Spirit of God working in us.

Should God's servants not be delighted to think that they have such a divine power working in them? Should they not yield with their whole hearts to its influence?

Oh, let us turn to the Master to give us, in the very depths of our hearts, the answer to the question, "Why could we not drive this evil spirit out?" He will say to our hearts, "It is because of your unbelief. You did not believe in Me and in the power of My Spirit, and with prayer and fasting seek for it."

You are called ...

"Come, follow Me," Jesus said,
"and I will make you fishers of men."
– Matthew 4:19

CHAPTER 6

The Supernatural

---

*I tell you the truth, anyone who has faith in Me will
do what I have been doing. He will do even greater
things than these, because I am going to the Father.*
                                             – John 14:12

Someone once said that, "Christianity is nothing if it is not supernatural." I agree with this
statement since it is only where this concept is
fully realized and acted on that the true church
can flourish. Let us try to understand what this
statement teaches us in connection with our review of the state of the church.

It teaches us, first of all, that Christianity is a
religion that came down from heaven and still
has to be unceasingly received from there. It is

ever dependent on the extent to which believers yield themselves to the immediate operation of the divine power.

Christianity points to God the Father and that unceasing action by which He works out everything according to the counsel of His will, even to its minutest detail. He is the God who "works all of them in all men" (1 Cor. 12:6).

It also points to Christ the Lord, to whom all power has been given, so that, just as He did His mighty works on earth, He may now live out and live over again in His people the life that He lived on earth. In the power of His resurrection, He will do even greater works than He did then (John 14:12). And Christianity points to the Holy Spirit, who proceeds unceasingly from the Father and the Son, who continuously works out in us God's plan according to His incomparably great power in us who believe (Eph. 1:19).

Just as Israel was brought out of Egypt by a mighty hand amid great and mighty wonders, so now the church is still upheld and guided by the omnipotent action of the triune God. This is not true just in regard to the great events of her history or the special interventions in her experience. It is likewise true in God's concern for every individual life, for all the work that is done from hour to hour by the feeblest of His servants.

Christianity is nothing if it is not, from beginning to end, through all and in all, the hidden, but direct and mighty energy of the living God continuing and working out the great redemption that He accomplished in His Son. Beyond all that He has given in creation and providence is that special working of the power of the divine life in its infinite holiness, which continuously works in us that likeness to Him that is pleasing in His sight.

"Christianity is nothing if it is not supernatural." There is even more meaning in this statement. We also learn from it what man's disposition and attitude ought to be toward God his Redeemer – absolute and unceasing dependence. The more we exercise faith in the revelation of the supernatural, as we have it in God's Word, the more we will learn that the first of our virtues should be a deep fear of God, a holy reverence in the presence of His glory, and a consciousness of our impotence under the sinful, accursed state that characterizes everything in creation.

Humility and a sense of nothingness is the posture that suits us. Faith in what God can do, will do, is always doing, and is waiting to do still more abundantly, becomes the unceasing habit of the soul, as unbroken in its continuity as the breathing of our lungs. What at first appeared to be a difficulty becomes a deep joy as we spontaneously surrender our hearts to the mighty working of God and His life within us.

To some, the supernatural may appear unnatural. That is simply because they have never understood how the supernatural may become, in the true sense, most natural. When we allow God to take perfect possession, the movements of our spiritual life can be as natural and joyous as our breathing.

However, for this we need the consciousness of how little our natural minds or hearts can take in this divine working. We need to learn that to know what the divine power can work in us is beyond the reach of human wisdom. The revelation of our redemption must be as supernatural as the redemption itself and its almighty action in our lives. From beginning to end, the work of grace is all, always, and in all things, the presence of God working and dwelling in us.

"Christianity is nothing if it is not supernatural." This statement teaches us still more. The more fully we yield ourselves to this statement, the more clearly we will discover that all the defects in our Christian lives and in the church around us are due to this one thing: We have not taken our true place before this glorious God so that He can work out in us what He has promised.

In the church this question is always coming up: What can be the reason that Christianity has so little true power and so little fulfills all the wonderful promises that it makes? Read all the discussions that are going on; notice carefully all the plans and efforts that are suggested for enabling the church to exercise the power it ought to have and to enable it to influence men, either the masses of nominal Christians or the millions of unbelievers around the world. All these thoughts and plans center on what man's wisdom can devise and what his zeal and energy can accomplish.

Everywhere, there is the thought that if believers will only keep up their courage and do their work faithfully, all must come out right.

How seldom do our ministers insist upon or stress the great truth that the Holy Spirit is our only power. An entire and absolute surrender to Him is our only hope. How seldom one hears from the church leaders, to whom the church looks for its guidance, the clear and unceasing summons: "Brothers, pray" (1 Thess. 5:25). We must pray more; we must "pray continually" (1 Thess. 5:17). Prayer will bring blessing. The measure of prayer is the measure of power.

Every deeper insight into what Christianity is, into what our daily life ought to be, into what the ministry is and needs, will lead us to one deep conviction: Christianity is nothing unless it is supernatural. Our Christian life and work will be a failure unless we live deeply rooted in the power of God's inspired Word, in the power of the Holy Spirit, and in the pressing prayer to which the promise of the Father will most surely be given.

All this brings us to our last lesson from this statement. There is no hope for the restoration of the church, no hope of her being lifted up into the abundant life that there is in Christ, no hope of her being equipped in holiness and strength for the work that is so urgently calling – that of making Christ known to every living individual – except in our return to God.

Church of Christ, give God His place! And take your place of absolute dependence, of unbroken fellowship, of unceasing prayer, of living, confident faith, and see if He will not turn and bless us above all that we can ask or think.

Someone has said, "The one real lack today is a lack of spiritual life; the one great need, the realization of the constant presence and power of the Holy Spirit." As we have already learned, "Back to divine wisdom, back to the living power of Jesus Christ, back through prayer to the source of all power" must be our motto.

The secret of all our strength for the work God has given us is absolute dependence on Him. God meant this to be an inconceivable privilege and honor. He intended for us to live in utter dependence on Him, just as His Son lived. Jesus, in fact, went to the grave to prove how surely God will work mightily for one who gives himself up completely to His will.

How strange that this concept of absolute dependence should cost us such trouble to understand and believe! Let the thought teach us our natural inability and incapacity for spiritual things, and bring us in a new surrender to accept the birthright that belongs to us as His children – the power of a divine life in Christ through the Spirit.

What we have seen of the state of the church, as revealed in her neglect and indifference to missions and her decline in membership, leads us to inquire as to the true cure of the evil condition. It is all comprised in one word – supernatural! Let us hold on to this thought as we continue exploring this topic.

We are naturally so inclined to listen to anything that calls us to take action, and so ready to undertake the fulfillment of divine commands in our own strength, that unless we are very careful, we may be deceived into putting our hope in what will turn out to be nothing but human devices.

Let us cultivate with our whole hearts a sense of God's power actively at work in us, an attitude of dependence and prayer and waiting on God, and a deep consciousness that God will work in us and in the church around us, above what we can ask or think. Then, the deeper we enter into the grievous need of the church and the world, the stronger will become our assurance that God is preparing us for deliverance.

However, remember the one condition – a habitual, unceasing, absolute dependence on Him. He must do all. He will do all for those who wait on Him.

You are called ...

To depend on what God can do,
will do, is always doing, and is
wanting to still do. As you do
so, your faith grows stronger.

CHAPTER 7

Christ's Last Words

You will receive power when the Holy Spirit comes on you; and you will be My witnesses in Jerusalem, and in all Judea and Samaria, and to the ends of the earth.

— Acts 1:8

When our Lord ascended to heaven, He left behind three last statements. The very last was, "You will be My witnesses ... to the ends of the earth" (Acts 1:8). Then we read, "After He said this, He was taken up" (v. 9). He left this world and His disciples with that one thought, "the ends of the earth."

A little while before this, He had said, "Go into all the world and preach the good news to all creation" (Mark 16:15). With that one thought in His heart, He sat down on the throne, longing for every child of man to learn to know Him and His love.

The second-to-last statement, which had just preceded the other, was, "You will receive power" (Acts 1:8). As He sent them forth for the conquest of the world, He told them not to think of their own weakness or their own strength. They were to think of all the power in heaven and on earth that He was now to receive from the Father. This power, through the Holy Spirit, would work in them and give them the victory.

Then we have the first of the three last statements: "Wait for the gift My Father promised" (Acts 1:4). In Luke's account, Jesus is recorded as saying, "Stay in the city until you have been clothed with the power from on high" (Luke 24:49). The disciples so clearly understood those words, "Wait," "Stay ... until" that they at once returned to the city. For ten days they continued with one accord in prayer and supplication, until, on the Day of Pentecost, they were indeed baptized with the heavenly fire and were all filled with the Holy Spirit and with power.

These three statements still express the relationship between Christ on the throne and His people. Just suppose for a moment that you were given the privilege of being caught up into paradise and of seeing and hearing what men may not know. You would, in the light and the power of that Spirit life, where words are eternally existing realities, be permitted to see the risen Lord on the throne, living with this one thought, "the ends of the earth," always in His heart, and always listening to the song of the redeemed from every people, nation and language.

How God waits and longs for the time when His love can reach every soul in the world. God loves the world; Christ gave His blood and His life for the world.

Moreover, you would know what a reality that second statement was, too, because you would see a Lamb standing, "looking as if it had been slain ... He had seven horns and seven eyes which are the seven spirits of God sent out into all the earth" (Rev. 5:6).

That holy symbol would show you how the Lamb on the throne lives to send forth God's Spirit wherever God's servants go, to enable them to make known His love and win souls for His kingdom.

You would also see the reality of the first of the three last statements, "Wait," which was interpreted by the disciples as a waiting that included much prayer and supplication. You would find there that:

The twenty-four elders fell down before the Lamb. Each one had a harp and they were holding golden bowls full of incense, which are the prayers of the saints. (Rev. 5:8)

The prayers of people here upon earth have their place and their part before the throne of God. You would see the smoke of the incense in the golden censer with the prayers of the saints going up before God. And you would understand what it is so hard for us to realize, that the prayers on earth are indeed the condition for receiving power from heaven to extend the kingdom on earth.

And if, in the vision, as you saw that it was passing, you felt bold to ask the Blessed One, "Do You have a message to give me for Your people on earth?" you would not be surprised if His answer came, "Tell them in My name to remember My last three statements. I carry the ends of the earth, for which I gave My blood and My love, in My heart. Let them do so, too.

"I live on the throne to send forth the Spirit into all the earth. Let them believe My promise, yield completely to My Spirit, and victory will certainly come. I am waiting to hear how much they are willing to have and to use; I am longing for more intercession and supplication, for more faith and prayer. Tell them to wait and keep on praying, and not to rest until they are clothed with power from on high. Tell them the kingdom and their Lord and King wait for their prayers."

Will we not take these last words of Christ afresh into our hearts? Has not God brought them home to us lately with a new meaning? Has not the terrible indictment against the home church – her lack of fitness or willingness to undertake the glorious, Christlike task of bringing God's love to every individual – pierced some hearts at least?

We have heard testimonies about the state of the church: her ignorance and her neglect and her rejection of the Cross, her lack of the sense of holiness and crucifixion to the world, her neglect of the blessed truth of the Holy Spirit, her lack of loyalty to the Lord Jesus, her terrible feebleness in prayer. Have not these testimonies become to some of us a burden that we cannot bear?

Will we not turn away from all our devices and efforts, and listen, with new, wholehearted devotion, to the great charter the church has too long neglected, the last statements of the ascending Lord? To take the words that live in Christ's heart and let them live in ours will be the secret of wonderful happiness and irresistible power.

"The ends of the earth." "All the world." "All creation." Is it possible for the ordinary Christian in everyday life to be so possessed by these words that, without effort or strain, they would be the spontaneous expression of his inmost life?

Thank God, it is possible, where the love of God and Christ is poured out into the heart. Poor, simple men and women have proved it by the intense devotion with which they could sacrifice everything to make the love of Jesus known to others.

The love with which Christ loves us is a love that takes in the whole world. Of that love we cannot take just enough for ourselves and be indifferent to all the others who share in it. Such is the feeble, selfish, and unhappy life that so many Christians seek to live.

In order to truly possess Christ and to fully enjoy Him, it is essential that we take in His love in all its fullness, that we yield ourselves to the service of that love, and that we find our happiness in making that love known to those who are still ignorant of it.

When the church is awakened and experiences in some measure the abundant life that there is in Christ Jesus, "the ends of the earth" will become her motto. People will begin to understand that what fills and satisfies the heart of Christ in heaven is enough and more than enough to fill our hearts with the blessedness and beauty of likeness to Him. "Remember," He says, "My very last statement, as I ascended the throne: 'You will be

My witnesses to the ends of the earth' (Acts 1:8)."

You will recall that the second-to-last statement was: "You will receive power, when the Holy Spirit comes on you" (v. 8). Yes, that is part of the last words of Christ: "the Holy Spirit." The Spirit of God was to be the divine empowerment that would carry them on irresistibly to universal conquest. He would sustain them through suffering and death, through long and patient labor, through many disappointments and trials. The victory was sure.

It has often been said that the Spirit flows from the Cross. The Spirit is inseparably linked to the Cross. In the fellowship of the Cross, they could always count on the fellowship of the Spirit and His almighty power.

But, alas, how soon the church began to shrink from the Cross and, without knowing it, began to lose that power of the Spirit, without which she is powerless to resist the power of the world.

Oh, that God would raise up believers who could, as with a trumpet voice, sound out this last statement of Christ: "You will receive power, when the Holy Spirit comes on you."

Oh, that God would raise up believers who could lead the church in returning to the Cross, with its crucifixion to the world, and in yielding herself to the glorious task of carrying the Cross in triumph to the ends of the earth. Let us implore our blessed Lord to write on our hearts this precious last phrase, too: "the Holy Spirit."

And then comes the first of the three last statements, "Wait" (Acts 1:4). The disciples spent their time of waiting in prayer and supplication. Church leaders have told us that:

> To multiply the number of Christians who will individually and collectively wield this force of intercession is the supreme question of foreign missions. Every other consideration is secondary to that of wielding the forces of prayer.

Jesus Christ in heaven waits for our prayers. The world's conquest waits for our prayers. It has been said, "The essential task of evangelizing the world is the lifting up of the church into a fuller spiritual life." This lifting up of the church waits for our prayers. Let us, above everything, implore God for the spirit of prayer.

Does not the Holy Spirit of God take the central place in these last instructions of Christ? Without faith in the promise of the Spirit, the church will fail in her duty, and lose the courage both to pray and to testify throughout all the earth.

Should not everyone who desires to live for Christ and His kingdom entreat God to remove the terrible blindness that hinders believers from seeing that there is just one thing lacking in the church's work – the power of the Spirit – and just one thing required – that the church fall down in intense, fervent prayer to wait until she is clothed with power from on high?

You are called ...

To tell the world that God loves the world; that Christ gave His blood and His life for the world.

CHAPTER 8

Early Christianity

> *Then the church throughout Judea, Galilee and Sa-*
> *maria enjoyed a time of peace. It was strengthened;*
> *and encouraged by the Holy Spirit, it grew in num-*
> *bers, living in the fear of the Lord.*
>
> — Acts 9:31

I n our last chapter we focused on the words of Christ, in which all God's power in heaven was promised to the church to enable it to fulfill the great task that Christ set before it. That power can be counted on in proportion to the measure of our faith and prayer. These questions natural-ly follow: How did the early church avail itself of that promise? Have we a right to expect its fulfill-ment in the same measure?

In his *Dawn on the Dark Continent*, Dr. Stewart compared the early church's missionary work with modern missionary work. He wrote:

The religious life of the early Christians seems to have possessed some vitality or concentrated spiritual power that helped Christianity, possibly because they believed intensely what they knew. Whatever it was, those Christians were successful as unofficial missionaries.

Dr Stewart further wrote:

In the early church its force and expansive power depended at first, as it still depends, on its internal condition, that is, on its spiritual life. The church of our day needs to be reminded that spiritual enterprises require spiritual conditions of the very highest force. And when the latter are lacking, the success desired may also be lacking.

I make no apology for dedicating the rest of this chapter to quoting a report entitled "The Missionary Message." It shows the difference between the amazing vitality of the early church and the comparative powerlessness of the church of our day.

Regaining the Power
of the Early Church

"There could have been no Pentecost had it not been for the life, death, and resurrection of the Son of God. These provided a revelation of God. The Cross revealed that He is absolute love and purity. The Resurrection revealed that He is absolute power. This revelation had to be given before the Spirit was given. Union with an impersonal absolute has in it no regenerative power; we need union with a personal God.

"When that revelation had been made, and when it had been accepted by the common faith of the church, Pentecost became divinely inevitable. The barriers of human resistance were broken at last, and the encompassing, waiting, besieging sea of the Spirit rushed in. At last the living Father, through the Son, had found receptive vessels, and therefore the Spirit was given.

From that point forward, believing men and women knew that no union with such a God could be too close and too steadfast. Their true life was hidden with Christ in God, and all true progress in it was progress within the absolute revelation.

"Is this too sweeping a statement as far as the Christian is concerned? Is it or is it not the view of the Christian revelation, that there is no limit to the efficacy of the Spirit of God in the life of man, except the measure of faith in those who receive it? Is it not true that all limitation and delay arise from the imperfect receptiveness of the Christian church?

"What is implied in God's promise to give His Spirit to the Christian church? How far can we count on God to sustain and transform us? How near can we come to Him within the conditions of time? How far is it true that He is still literally creative in His world whenever and wherever He finds faith? Are there in Him unimagined resources of life simply awaiting the rise of faith, just as the riches of nature throughout the ages awaited the discovery and development of science?

"When we endeavor to explain the difference between the amazing vitality of the early church and the comparative powerlessness of today's church, three possible explanations suggest themselves.

"The first starts from existing facts and endeavors to explain the early records in the light of present attainment. This view says that the standard of judgment is the church as we know it, and that the actual life of the heroic age could not have differed in any real degree from the present church.

"The second view is that these records of the first one hundred and fifty years of the church's life are true history. The contrast between the spiritual exaltation and achievement of that age and the comparative depression of our own lies in the fact that, for wise and good reasons, God has restricted the early gift of the Spirit and put us under a more rigid and limited dispensation.

"The third view, like the second, holds to the truth of the records, but explains the difference between the early centuries and our own by saying that, while God remains unchanging in His grace, the church has failed to comply with the conditions of receiving it.

Faith, according to this view, has gradually become depressed, and so the church has lost the expectancy that is the condition of all spiritual achievement.

"Why have our prayers failed to overcome the remaining sin and tragedy in the Christian life? According to this third view, it is because the common faith and love of the church is far below the common faith and love of early days. The individual who lacks this faith and love cannot attain the ancient summit.

The true remedy for such failure does not lie in abandoning the enterprises of faith as hopeless, while blaming the failure on God, but in flinging all our energies into the task of rousing the slumbering life of the church. We must awaken it to a new community of faith and love, and press on from there to new personal attainment.

"This view argues that the idea of God having restricted our spiritual resources has no foundation in revelation. Revealed truth declares that believers everywhere may count on the Spirit of God with the same assurance, as they rest on the unchanging providence of God.

It also proves that, whether it is recognized or not, the whole missionary movement of the nineteenth century rested on a different foundation than ours. It began with William Carey's, 'Expect great things from God; attempt great things for God.' And its progress since then has been measured by the degree of expectancy, which again has depended on the depth and strength and grandeur of its idea of God.

"Is the delay in the coming of the divine kingdom due to a lowering of the common faith of the church – a lapse of ages of time, a lapse as wide as the Christendom of the modern world? Are there unseen around us today all the forces of the Divine Spirit that surrounded the first ages? Do they await only the rise of a generation stronger in faith and love than our own?

"If so, then clearly the one true attitude for the church is to confess its historic sin and get ready for the most resolute and strenuous endeavor and prayer. Then the numbing mists of our common unbelief may be dispelled. Then the redeeming will of God in Christ may have free course in blessing the entire life of man.

"If this third view is true, we have been attributing to the inscrutable will of God innumerable temporal and spiritual evils that are really the result of our fostering thoughts of God that are unworthy of His goodness, wisdom, and power. In this case, our whole perspective of God is being lowered and darkened by a false theory of His ways with people.

"Are the same divine resources available today as in the early ages? The church is once more facing its duty to the whole world. It has been led by the providence and the Spirit of God into circumstances that are taxing her resources to the limit. Everywhere the question of our resources is coming to the forefront.

"But there is surely common agreement that behind all these things there is an incomparably deeper need.

Behind all questions of quantity lies the incomparably weighty question of quality. It is not simply the spiritual quality of our missionaries that is the crucial point; it is the spiritual quality of the church that is behind them. It is the spiritual character of the great masses of common Christians – their faith, their love, their hopes, their reception of the power of the Spirit.

"A question arises and presses for an answer: At this moment, does the church possess the spiritual resources for reaching the world? Or, like Israel in the days of the prophets, is her existing spiritual attainment insufficient for the great world emergency that has broken upon her?"

Valuable Lessons

How we need to learn these lessons from "The Missionary Message." With what force all the lessons that we need at this time are taught.

Seeking and finding the supernatural power of the Holy Spirit is the one condition of success in the work of Christ's kingdom.

That power, as it manifested itself in the early church, is available for the church today. All the feebleness from which the church is suffering, in her decline of membership and in her inability to fulfill her calling, can have no other cause but the lack of the presence and power of the Holy Spirit in her ministries.

How inconceivable that the church does not know and act upon the blessed truth that the Holy Spirit will work in her all that she needs of the divine strength for winning the world.

The plea for more prayer opens the certain path to the power of the Spirit in every work the church has to do.

You are called ...

To this you were called, because Christ suffered for you, leaving you an example, that you should follow in His steps.

– 1 Peter 2:21

CHAPTER 9

Seven Times More Prayer

During the days of Jesus' life on earth, He offered up prayers and petitions with loud cries and tears to the one who could save Him from death, and He was heard because of His reverent submission.

– Hebrews 5:7

I took part in the World Missionary Conference and the reports that followed the conference greatly stress the supreme importance of prayer. I will begin this chapter with some excerpts from these reports:

Prayer is the method that links the irresistible might of God to the missionary enterprise. That God has conditioned so largely the extension and the fruitfulness of His kingdom upon the faithfulness and loyalty of His children in prayer is, at the same time, one of the deepest mysteries and one of the most wonderful realities.

That paragraph is worth reading again. Here is another:

How to multiply the number of Christians who, with clear and unshakable faith in the character and ability of God, will wield this force for the transformation of man – that is the supreme question of foreign missions. Every other consideration is secondary to that of wielding the forces of prayer. May the call go forth from this conference to the Christian churches throughout the world to give themselves as never before to intercession.

An entire chapter of one report is devoted to prayer, and especially the need of education in prayer. Here are a few paragraphs from that chapter:

It is our conviction that none can pray their best, and few can pray with any fullness of effect, who have not received some careful training in the practice of prayer and have not acquired as well the grace of holy perseverance in it.

We must emphasize the fact that encouraging

and directing the prayer of Christian people is one of the highest forms of Christian service.

We take for granted that those who love this work and carry it upon their hearts will follow the Scripture's admonition to pray unceasingly for its triumph. To such, all times and seasons will witness an attitude of intercession that refuses to let God go until He crowns His workers with victory.

Prayer is the putting forth of vital energy. It is the highest effort of which the human spirit is capable. Effectiveness and power in prayer cannot be obtained without patient continuance and much practice. The primary need is not the multiplication of prayer meetings, but that individual Christians should learn to pray.

The secret and art of prayer can only be learned from the teaching of the Master Himself, and by patient study of the best books on the subject.

Sometimes it has seemed as if faith in the power of the Spirit and in His willingness to aid had been almost lost, and that we were now attempting to substitute human devices for spiritual power. All plans to deepen interest in missionary work must be devised and executed in devout prayer and solemn waiting upon the Lord.

These are indeed unspeakably solemn words. They lead us into the depth of the sanctuary. They open up to us the divine meaning and mystery of prayer as very few understand them. They call us to entreat God by His Holy Spirit to open our eyes so that we may know what prayer is in its spiritual reality.

Most Christians are content if they have some blessed experience of what prayer can do in bringing down blessings for their own needs, and maybe for the needs of others. Yet, how seldom it is realized that prayer covers the whole divine mystery of man being in partnership with the triune God in working out the counsel of His will and grace.

All that God wants to do for the world, He does through people whom He has taken into His counsel. These people have yielded themselves fully to His will. His Spirit has taken possession of them so that they can pray with power in the name of Jesus. Such have the high honor that God will regulate the working of His Holy Spirit at their request. He will send His Spirit to go where and to do what they have asked.

This is indeed the mystery of prayer, that worms of the dust can become members of God's private council. The Holy One listens to such and becomes the executor of their plans and wishes. Prayer brings forth the infinite and omnipotent resources of God, and God's saints have the honor of praying. No wonder the chapter from which I have been quoting concludes with these words:

If the conference should lead some resolutely and irrevocably to enter into the school of prayer, the spiritual power of the church for the accomplishment of its great task would be immeasurably increased.

Now, how do all these excerpts relate to the state of the church? First of all, they should deepen the painful conviction of how little the church knows how to pray and how unfit most of its members are to pray effectively.

We need time to get a full impression of what the Christian life means to most people, even those who are considered earnest. They have been taught to come to Christ for their salvation. They have found it, and they now seek to live in the world, looking to God for enough grace to enable them to live what they think are Christian lives.

They have no conception of the claim Christ has to an entire consecration of their whole being. They have no idea that it is definitely their great calling to live to make Christ king throughout the earth. The thought is entirely foreign to them that every day of their lives they are to pray, to labor in prayer, so that God's kingdom may come and so that God's Spirit may use them for His service.

When we compare this attitude with Scripture, the charge is brought home to us that the church is feeble and utterly unable to strive in prayer for the conversion of the world. I implore my readers to look back over all the excerpts in this chapter to see what ought to be, and what is not found to be, until the prayerlessness of the church becomes a burden too heavy to be borne.

After considering these things, the true Christian must surrender at once. He must wholly yield himself to become an intercessor.

When speaking of the work that needs to be done, Dr. Robson used this expression: "We will need three times more men, four times more money, seven times more prayer." That is, instead of twenty thousand men, we now need sixty thousand men; instead of ten million dollars, now forty million; instead of the amount of prayer being offered, now seven times more prayer.

If a congregation had at present three laborers in the field, it would not be impossible, if the right spirit prevailed, to increase that number to nine. If there were a Christian man who had given five percent of his income to foreign missions, it would surely not be too much, if a right sense of the claim of Christ came upon him, for him to give four times that amount – twenty percent. Would it then be thought impossible to believe that, when God's Spirit even now begins to work in the hearts of God's children, they will be drawn into seven times more prayer?

It is not only that we want the number of those who pray to be greatly increased, but even more we desire that those who already pray would accept the call for their part in the sevenfold. Quality is more important than quantity. Sevenfold is the sign of the quiet perseverance of Elijah that would not rest until the cloud had been seen. Sevenfold is the sign of the burning furnace seven times heated. Our hope lies in the new intensity of the prayer of those who already pray.

Christ "offered up prayers and petitions with loud cries" (Heb. 5:7), but He first offered Himself. Offer yourself to God, and a new power will come to offer up prayer without ceasing. Begin at once. Take each chapter of this book, and turn it into prayer. Take up the great subjects, and just speak your heart in communion with God. Again, go back to the quotations I have given. Make them food for prayer until your heart begins to understand what it means to give God no rest until He pours down His blessing.

There is an even more important message in these excerpts. They first refer to prayer for foreign missions. However, this book has to do with a subject on which missions is absolutely dependent – the spiritual life of the church. I included the excerpts to rouse the hearts of Christians to unceasingly pray for a revival. Without it, the church can never respond to the call of her Lord.

We may pray for the church at large, the church to which we belong, or the circle with which we are more closely linked. Regardless, let our prayer for missions lift up to God our first and primary desire – that His believing children who have known what prayer is may be stirred to a new intensity.

That will lead them to ask that His feebler children may take courage and confidently expect Him to give them the Spirit of supplication, too.

Then will follow the prayer that His wandering children, who profess to trust in Christ but have never thought of what it is to live for His service, may, by the mighty movement of His grace, be brought to take their part in the great army of intercessors. In the ministry of intercession they will cry to Him day and night until He avenges them of their adversary (Luke 18:3).

May God find His people ready for it.

You are called ...

To pray effectively, intensely and without
ceasing. All that God wants to do for the world,
He does through people who pray.

CHAPTER 10

A Holiness Revival

*In Your unfailing love You will lead the people You
have redeemed. In Your strength You will guide them
to Your holy dwelling.*

– Exodus 15:13

How is the church to be lifted to the level of
abundant life in Christ? How can she gain
the vitality that will prepare her for the work that
God is putting before her?

In answer to these questions, many will without hesitation say, "Nothing will help but a revival." Indeed, that alone is the something that
must happen to the church.

As Mr. Oldham put it:

If the World Missionary Conference had any meaning at all, it disclosed a situation so serious that nothing less than a tremendous spiritual revival can be adequate to meet it. It is a new and living understanding of God and of His purpose for the world that we seem most of all to need if there is to be an irresistible spiritual movement. Such a movement is the only thing adequate to the needs of the situation. Great tides of spiritual energy must be set in motion if the work is to be accomplished.

Yes, all perceptive believers will conclude that nothing less than a mighty revival is needed. Nothing less will rouse and prepare the church for the work to which God calls her.

Yet, there may be great differences in what is understood by "revival." Many will think of the power of God as it has been manifested in the work of evangelists like D. L. Moody and R. A. Torrey. They feel sure that what God has done in the past He can do again. They will perhaps hardly be able to understand me when I say that we need a different and a mightier revival than those were.

In those revivals, the chief purpose was the conversion of sinners and, in connection with that, the reviving of believers. But the revival that we need calls for a deeper and more entire upheaval of the church. The great defect of those revivals was that the converts were received into a church that was not living on a high level of consecration and holiness, and they quickly sank down to the average standard of ordinary religious life. Even believers who had taken part in the work and had been stirred by it also gradually returned to their former life of clouded fellowship and lack of power to testify for Christ.

The revival we need is the revival of holiness. In this kind of revival, the consecration of one's whole being to the service of Christ for the rest of one's life is considered possible. For this we will need a new style of preaching, in which the promises of God to dwell in His people and to sanctify them for Himself will take a place that they do not now have.

Let me try to make this plain by an illustration from the history of Israel. When God redeemed His people from Egypt by the blood of the Passover and the deliverance at the Red Sea, this was only a beginning of what He intended to do. He had a higher purpose and a fuller blessing for them. He meant to dwell among them as the Holy One and to be their God. He meant to sanctify them as His people.

We find this twofold aim in the song of Moses: "In Your unfailing love You will lead the people You have redeemed" (Exod. 15:13). That was the wonderful beginning. Then, "In Your strength You will guide them to Your holy dwelling" (v. 13).

Just as God had said to Moses, "I am the LORD, and I will bring you out from under the yoke of the Egyptians ... And I will bring you to the land" (Exod. 6:6, 8), the redemption from Egypt was only the foundation. The house to be built on it was the sanctuary, in which God dwelt in the midst of His people as the Holy One, to make them holy, too. Yet, there were many Israelites who were brought out from bondage but were never brought into rest. They perished in the wilderness through unbelief.

When our Lord Jesus, in His farewell discourse, gave the promise of the Holy Spirit, He spoke of the new covenant blessing that would then be experienced: God dwelling in His people.

> "If anyone loves Me, he will obey My teaching. My Father will love him, and we will come to him and make our home with him." (John 14:23)

Paul wrote the words, "That Christ may dwell in your hearts through faith ... that you may be filled to the measure of all the fullness of God" (Eph. 3:17, 19). Dr. Maclaren has said that it seems as if the thought of Christ dwelling in our hearts has been lost in the church. In the Reformation, the great truth of justification – the bringing out from the bondage of Egypt – was restored to its place. But the other great truth of sanctification – the bringing into the land with its rest and victory – has never yet taken the place in the preaching and practice of the church that God's Word claims for it.

It is for this that we need a revival, that the Holy Spirit may so take possession of us that the Father and the Son can live in us, and that fellowship with them, and devotion to their will and service, will be our chief joy. This will indeed be a holiness revival.

A holiness revival! Has there ever been such a thing? There have been movements in the church that, though they have not been known by that name, have resulted in definite and intense consecration to God and His will. There have also been fuller manifestations of the Spirit that have left their marks in history. Many church leaders say that the Moravian ideal is what the church ought to aim at – every member ready for the work of the Kingdom.

The Moravian community owed its birth to a true holiness revival. There were gathered together at Herrnhut, a small religious community, a number of refugees from Bohemia, along with a number of Christians of different groups, who hoped to find the Christian life as they sought for it. It was not long before disputes arose, and Herrnhut became a scene of contention and division.

Nikolaus von Zinzendorf felt this so deeply that he went down to live among them. In the power of God's Spirit, he succeeded not only in restoring order, but in binding them together in the power of devotion to Jesus and love for each other.

More than once they had remarkable manifestations of the presence of the Spirit, and their whole life became one of worship and praise. After they had been having nightly fellowship meetings for a couple of years, they were led to consecrate the whole community to the service of Christ's kingdom.

When John Wesley visited them, he wrote as follows:

> God has given me at length the desire of my heart. I am with a church whose conversation is in heaven, in whom is the mind that was in Christ, and who so walk as He walked. Here I continually meet with what I sought for – living proofs of the power of faith, persons saved from inward as well as outward sin by the love of God shed abroad in their hearts. I was extremely comforted and strengthened by the conversation of this lovely people.

It was in a holiness revival that the Moravian missionary idea was born and realized.

A holiness revival! What was the great evangelical revival in England through George Whitefield and John Wesley but this? They had together at Oxford been members of "The Holy Club." With their whole hearts they had sought to live for God, to keep themselves separate from the world, to devote their lives to the welfare of their fellowmen.

They had not only sought deliverance from the guilt, but also from the power of sin. When their eyes were opened to see how faith can claim the whole Christ in all His fullness, they found the key to the preaching that was so mightily effective for the salvation of sinners.

What John Wesley did for the Methodists, General William Booth, as his disciple, did for the Salvation Army. Looking at the material with which he had to work, it is amazing how he inspired tens of thousands with a true devotion to Christ and to the lost. He accomplished this with his teaching of a clean heart and a full salvation.

If I remember correctly, one noted church historian has said that, along with Spurgeon, John Wesley and General Booth are among those whom God has most honored for winning many souls for Christ. Such a testimony has all the greater value because I know how far that particular scholar is from agreeing with the teaching of holiness as these men thought they had found it in God's Word.

There may be great differences of doctrine, but no one can be blind to the seal God has set upon the intense desire to preach a full and entire consecration.

A revival of holiness is what we need. We need a preaching about Christ's claim on us that will lead us to live entirely for Him and His kingdom.

We need an attachment of love to Him that will make His fellowship our highest joy.

We need a faith in His ability to free us from sin's dominion that will enable us to obey His commandments in all things.

We need a yielding to the Holy Spirit that will cause us to be led by Him in our entire daily walk.

These will be some of the elements of a revival of true holiness. The church must learn to seek for this revival as for the "pearl of great value" (Matt. 13:45-46).

And how is it to be found? It will cost much prayer. It will cost more than that – much sacrifice of self and of the world. It will require a surrender to Christ Jesus to follow Him as closely as God is able to work it in us. We must learn to look at a life like Christ's as the supreme goal of daily life. We must have the very same mind that was in Christ.

May the prayer of the Scottish preacher Robert Murray McCheyne become ours: "Lord, make me as holy as a pardoned sinner can be." May it be offered by an increasing number of ministers and believers. Then the promise of the new covenant will become a matter of experience.

We need to hear preaching about God in His holiness, about Christ as our sanctification, and about the work of the Spirit as the Spirit of holiness. When this preaching takes the place that it has in God's Word, God's people will have the power to do the work to which God has called them – making Christ known to every living individual.

This promise will then be fulfilled: "The nations will know that I am the LORD, declares the Sovereign LORD, when I show Myself holy through you before their eyes." (Ezek. 36:23).

You are called ...
Just as He who called you is
holy, so be holy in all you do.
– 1 Peter 1:15

CHAPTER 11

Christ's Claim upon Us

> *Jesus Christ, who gave Himself for us to redeem us from all wickedness and to purify for Himself a people that are His very own, eager to do what is good.*
>
> – Titus 2:13-14

Indifference to missionary work prevails. The cause, many say, is that Christians are utterly unconscious of the claim Christ has on them. At conversion, their attention was directed to salvation from punishment, along with grace to help them to a better life.

The thought that Christ had purchased them as a people of His own, "eager to do what is good" (Titus 2:14), that through them He might from heaven continue and carry on the work He had begun on earth, never entered their minds. They knew that they ought to do good works as the proof of their love, but they never understood that these good works were service that Christ actually needed for the extension of His kingdom. They did not know that their whole lives, with all their abilities, were to be at His disposal for that purpose.

If there is to be a deep missionary revival, it will have to begin here: God's children who are striving to serve Him must get a new and far deeper insight into the blessedness of this claim of Christ.

God wants them to be able to tell of it and to testify about the source of their motivation. They can pass on a power that will rouse Christians who have been living the selfish life. Selfish Christians will be roused to a new thought that they never had before – the real blessedness of belonging to Christ. Only in this way will the world know that the love of God, in heavenly measure and power, dwells in Christians.

May God, by His Holy Spirit, open our eyes to see what this wonderful claim of Christ means.

What is the ground upon which it rests? That He is our God and Creator? This is only the beginning of it, and its power has been so obliterated by sin that something else was needed. And what a stupendous miracle was accomplished when the Son of God came to earth to unite Himself with us in all our sin and suffering. He not only suffered, but also endured the judgment of a Holy God, which we deserved.

Yes, so completely did He identify Himself with us that He stooped to bear our curse. He gave His life and His blood on our behalf. And He made us eternally one with Himself in His resurrection and ascension and in the glory into which He entered upon the throne of God. We are so completely one with Him that throughout the whole universe we will be known as His body, the inseparable companion and sharer of His place in the heart of the Father.

What is the ground on which Christ's claim rests? We need to think about Christ's sacrifice if this question is to be answered with a power that compels the heart. Is He not worthy of having your every thought and every ability yielded to Him – to be His completely and His alone?

That gives us the answer to the second question: What really is Christ's claim? It is nothing less than this: We should give ourselves for Him and to Him as completely as He gave Himself for us and to us.

In chapter two, I used the expression, "The measure of the surrender of Christ for us and our salvation, is the measure of our surrender to Him and to His service." This is an expression I cannot forget although I cannot grasp it. This same idea was expressed by Dr. Denney:

> We must seek to persuade men that a love like Christ's can only be answered by a love in kind, and that, for a Savior who came not only in water but in blood, there can be no adequate response that is bloodless. There must be a passion in the answer of our souls that reciprocates the passion of His love to us.

As we take in these words, we will begin to understand Christ's claim on us. He lived on earth, and now lives in heaven, in the fullness of a love for us that surpasses knowledge. In the same way, nothing can now satisfy His heart, or our own, but a love that on our part seeks to live every moment in His presence and for His pleasure.

Just as His love showed itself in a life of intense and unceasing action, so our love must be ready to wait on His will and to place our abilities at His disposal.

We should be constantly on the lookout to see, not how much we can manage to keep for ourselves, but what else we can find to give Him who has given His all so unreservedly for us.

There will then be no need for pleading for missionaries or for money. A group that loves

Him will eagerly offer anything that the Master may desire.

Now comes the third question: How can we have the power to yield to Christ's claim and live in unbroken surrender to it? The thought comes readily to mind that it may be a very beautiful ideal, but how impossible it is to carry it out. Listen to Christ's answer: He Himself undertakes to settle all claims that He has upon us.

The love that gave itself on the Cross, with the one thought of getting complete possession of us, is the love that in all its intensity and power watches over and works in us every hour of the day. When He gave Himself for us, He gave Himself to us. Surely a lost sheep can count on its strong shepherd to carry it back to its home. No less can each one of us count on the whole Christ, and count on Him constantly, to carry us. He is entirely ready to keep us from sin and to work out in us all "in accordance with His pleasure and will" (Eph. 1:5).

Some ask the question, but why do we experience so little of His power? The answer is simple. We do not know it, we do not believe it, we do not yield ourselves to it. The limited action of the Holy Spirit, hindered as He is by the spirit of the world, is the one cause of our failure. Christ calls for a passion of love toward Him that corresponds to His toward us.

No power but His own love, dwelling in the heart and working there, can for a moment think of giving what He claims. He Himself, by His abiding presence, by His indwelling Spirit, by His unceasing working in us, must do all.

And this brings us to the fourth great question: How can a soul who longs to yield himself wholly to Christ's claim, make good his claim on Christ Himself to carry out all His work in us? The answer is simple and yet beyond the power of the human mind to fully grasp.

Nothing less is needed than that the Spirit should glorify Christ in His claim on us and in our claim on Him. It is when we see how impossible it is for a person to really know and love Christ that we will come in our helplessness and cast ourselves at His feet. Then we will believe in the power of His Word to work in us a full faith in Him and all He has done and will do.

As we turn away from the world and from self and consent to be crucified with Him, we will find, in the fellowship of His death, the power through which He conquers sin. We will find, in the fellowship of His resurrection, the heavenly life through which He dwells in us, becomes one with us, and works out all His blessed purpose.

True love cannot rest until, by its divine power, it possesses the heart of the beloved one. God's love draws our love to itself and does not rest until our love has perfectly responded.

And now, this claim of Christ must be proclaimed in the church with a new power from on high. Who should proclaim it? It should be those who have yielded themselves wholly to it, who have given their lives here at home to let Christ work in them all that He wills. It should be those who are seeking with their whole hearts, even in the midst of conscious imperfection, to see Christ's claim fully acknowledged in the church.

When such believers begin to give themselves to prayer and supplication so that it might happen, hearts will begin to be touched. Christians, whether ministers or not, will begin to understand. They will see that for such an unspiritual, powerless church to be roused for the great work of making Christ's claim known to unbelievers around the world, nothing less is needed than the mighty power of the Spirit ruling in the hearts and lives of God's children.

And every thought of the state of the home church and the crying need of the non-Christian world will be swallowed up in this one thought: Christ claims the world, and Christ expects everyone who has learned that claim to yield himself wholly to it and to live only to make it known.

CHAPTER 12

The Promise of the Father

---

*If you then, though you are evil, know how to give
good gifts to your children, how much more will your
Father in heaven give the Holy Spirit to those who
ask Him!*

— Luke 11:13

The Holy Spirit is the promise of the Father.
That promise includes everything we need.
In order to truly know God, in order to experience and enjoy all that Christ is and has for us, in
order to possess the true and full life that a child
of God may expect even here on earth – everything depends on our being possessed and filled
with the Holy Spirit of God.

We are absolutely dependent on the abundant

measure of the Spirit that God is so willing to give and that He promises to give. Everything that reminds us of the fallen state of the church, of her unfaithfulness and lack of loyalty to Christ, of the terrible power that the world has over her, of her powerlessness to carry out her mission here on earth, is just another call: "If you had responded to My rebuke, I would have poured out My heart to you" (Prov. 1:23).

Ignorance prevails concerning Christ's cross and the holiness it offers. Christian ministers and workers are content to struggle on in their human efforts to save sinners. They do not give the Holy Spirit the first place that He must have.

In view of all this, let us once again listen to the great promise that Christ gave His disciples when He was teaching them to pray. Let us see whether our hearts will not yield to this wonderful promise and turn to God for what He will so surely give.

Listen now to the promise of the Father:

If you then, though you are evil, know how to give good gifts to your children, how much more will your Father in heaven give the Holy Spirit to those who ask Him! (Luke 11:13)

In these words we find four deep and unfathomable mysteries. First, the mystery of the Holy

Spirit whom God offers to give us. Second, the mystery of the Father's infinite willingness to give that gift. Third, the mystery of the Son of God, who came from heaven to bring the promise and to open the way for its fulfillment, and who now from heaven is the channel through whom the Father gives it. And fourth, the mystery of prayer, by which that great gift can be drawn down upon ourselves and others.

If it were to please God to open our eyes fully to see the glory of these mysteries, we could not for a moment hesitate to give up everything to have the promise fulfilled in us.

The Holy Spirit

First is the inconceivable mystery of the gift of the Holy Spirit. Who is He? He is the Spirit of God. Just as a man has his life in the spirit that animates his body, the whole life and glory of the Deity is contained in the Holy Spirit.

The Spirit is the bond of union between the Father and the Son. He is the Spirit of the Father and of the Son, too. And this very same Spirit is to be the Spirit of our lives, dwelling in us as the hidden God, doing His work to reveal the Son and the Father within us. The Spirit of God dwells and works in us! The thought is so overwhelming that it compels us to worship and adore.

God has said that this blessed Spirit will be the life of our lives. He is given with the express purpose of working out in us all that God wants us to be and to do. He is given with the understanding that we never need to do in our own strength what God commands. The Spirit will work it in us.

He comes as the whole God to take possession of the whole man. He will be responsible for the whole of our lives if we will yield ourselves to Him in faith. He will glorify Christ in us. As we look up to Christ, and through Him to the Father, the blessed Spirit will work in the depth of our hearts the likeness of God and His Christ.

The Father's Willingness

Now let us examine the second mystery, the mystery of the Father's inconceivable willingness to give this infinite gift. "How much more will your Father in heaven give the Holy Spirit to those that ask Him?" (Luke 11:13). Christ takes an illustration from the deepest experience of our daily lives.

Have we not, as children, learned to know and trust and rejoice in the willingness of a father to give us the food we need? How natural, how easy, what joy it was, to live in that assurance of what a father would do!

Now, just think of what this phrase means: "How much more will your Father in heaven ... " Think of His greatness. Think of His holiness. Think of His love and His tender compassion. Then say, "Do we not have good reason for the most unbounded confidence? The Father is just longing to fill us with His Holy Spirit." Oh, the mystery of this inconceivable longing of God to give us His Holy Spirit! Take time to take it in.

If He is so willing, why, then, do we so often pray and have to wait a long time for the answer? It is simply that *we* are not willing. We hinder Him.

We do not yield our whole hearts and souls, our entire beings. We are not like a hungry child, for a hungry child will certainly be fed by his father. We are not ready to sacrifice everything and seek only what the Father longs to give.

Let us believe in the mystery of the Father's willingness to give the Spirit. It will draw us to come closer to God and, under the power of His love, to lay ourselves at His feet.

The Son of God

The third mystery involves the One who brings this wonderful message. It is no one less than the Son of God. As if to make unbelief impossible, God sent His only begotten Son as the bearer of the good tidings. He came to prepare the way to deliver us from the power of sin. He came to yield His own body as a living sacrifice on the cross, so that He might then receive the Spirit from the Father to impart to us.

Sin had so separated us and our whole beings from God that it was only by death to the old nature, death to sin, that a new creation could be formed in which the Holy Spirit could dwell.

Here we have the reason why, in spite of the infinite willingness of God to give the Spirit, we find it so difficult to receive Him. It is only through Christ's death on the cross that He is able to impart to us the full power of the Holy Spirit when we come into fellowship with Him and His death.

It is when we are crucified with Him to the world, and when we live in Him as those who are dead to sin, that He can do His blessed work in us.

The Power of Prayer

The fourth mystery is the inconceivable power of my feeble prayer to draw down the Holy Spirit from heaven to work where and what I ask in the name of Jesus.

Not only will the Father give me the Spirit, but He will send the Spirit at my request to other souls near me, and in far-distant lands. Yes, this is what prayer has done and is doing today. This is what it will do far more abundantly when God's children learn to believe the promise and take hold of His strength.

It is high time for the church to stop looking at prayer only in the light of our feebleness or our limited desires. We must begin to believe that God, in the mystery of prayer, has entrusted us with a force that can move the heavenly world and bring its power down to this earth.

The prayer of one hundred and twenty at Pentecost brought down the power of the promised Spirit. When the church continues to be "together constantly in prayer" (Acts 1:14), the kingdom of heaven will again come down in power into the hearts and lives of people. We cannot begin to conceive the extent of this at the present time.

The Proper Response

Take time to seriously consider these four mysteries: the gift of the Holy Spirit, the infinite willingness of the Father to give Him, the blessed Son who is the channel, and the inconceivable power of the prayer of faith!

Let each of us ask and receive for himself. Yes, let us believe with our whole hearts that God gives, gives every day afresh, and gives in increasing power His blessed Spirit to every child who asks in a right manner.

Let each of us believe in the power of prayer to bring the blessing to others. Let us cry to God continually that His children may learn to believe in His blessed promise and to live in the power of it.

As we think of what has been called "this Spiritless age," and the low state of spiritual life in the church, and the terrible need of the world, let us especially yield ourselves to the work of intercession.

Let us allow the Holy Spirit to make us into believers who cry to God day and night until He pours out His blessed Spirit so that there is not enough room to receive Him.

Let every prayer breathe the confident assurance, "How much more will your Father in heaven give the Holy Spirit to those that ask Him?" (Luke 11:13).

Seeking the Spirit

In *The Decisive Hour of Missions*, Dr. John Mott wrote:

The Reverend J. Goforth bears testimony that the results of the different evangelistic missions were in direct proportion to the extent the missionaries and Chinese Christians yielded themselves to God and sought the power of the Holy Spirit.

He expresses the conviction that, "if the church of Christ will humble itself under the hand of God, the Holy Spirit will confirm the preaching of the Word with unmistakable signs of His presence and power.

I have the strongest of convictions that it would pay much, even manifold, for the church at home and abroad to cease for a season its busy round of activities and seek for the Holy Spirit's power as for hidden treasure. If we want to evangelize the world in our day, we must get back to the Pentecostal factor."

The church professes to believe that the Holy Spirit is the mighty power of God, that He will be given in answer to believing, persevering prayer, and that He will clothe His ministers with power from on high.

Yet, the church does not avail itself of this great promise and does not consider much prayer for the Holy Spirit as the first and all-important thing in the work of saving sinners. Is this not incomprehensible?

Our faith in the Holy Spirit is, to a great extent, simply intellectual. If it were not, we would count it our greatest privilege to ask and to receive the

Holy Spirit in doing God's work. It would be impossible for us not to.

In order to do God's work, let us seek the power of the Holy Spirit.

You are called ...

Therefore, holy brothers,
who share in the heavenly calling,
fix your thoughts on Jesus, the apostle
and high priest whom we confess.
– Hebrews 3:1

CHAPTER 13

A Token of God's Displeasure

These are the words of him who holds the seven spirits of God and the seven stars. I know your deeds; you have a reputation of being alive, but you are dead.

– Revelation 3:1

As we read in chapter two, the following words were spoken by Dr. Denney in reference to his own denomination. Unfortunately, these same words likewise apply to many other churches and many other denominations. I have expanded his comments in this chapter. Read his words carefully:

I speak only of the denomination to which I myself belong, but something similar I believe is true of every church in Christendom. My denomination has 1700 congregations, and during the last five years the increase in its membership has been about 850 members. That is to say, every second congregation has added one member, and every other congregation has added none.

The number of candidates for the ministry is much smaller at the present time than it was a good many years ago. It is hardly a sufficient number to keep up the staff at home, to say nothing of supplying workers abroad. People are not coming forward as ministers, nor are they coming forward as missionaries, because they are not coming forward into the membership of the Christian church at all. Something must happen to the church at home if it is going to even look at the work that has been put upon it [in foreign missions].

Just think of an insurance company, or any secular business, counting up the clients that it has gained through its agents during a year. What would it do if it received a report like the one the church has received? There would be an urgent order at once for a thorough investigation. Then there would be a review of all the methods and agents responsible for the decrease.

And what can be the reason in the church of Christ that this process of decrease has been allowed to go on? In his complete comments from which this excerpt was taken, Dr. Denney spoke of people who will not part with money or pleasure for the good of the church. Then he said, "I say the world is full of people like that, and what is worse, whoever is to blame for it, the church is full of them, too."

In every investigation in connection with a business undertaking, the aim is to lay the blame on the guilty one. Who is to blame here? The ministry as a whole? The individual ministers who are responsible for the decline? The congregations who, by their worldliness and lack of spiritual life, hinder the ministers? Or, the governing bodies of the church, because they have allowed things to come to such a crisis without sounding the alarm in the ears of the ministers and people?

We have asked questions that we do not know how to answer. Only God knows fully who is to blame. But God is willing to give us the courage and the honesty to find out and make confession, each on his own behalf, of what share we have had in this sad condition of the flock of Christ.

But apart from the question of blame, there is still the deeper question concerning the spiritual significance of the situation.

What is the cause of the decline? Is it that the gospel has not been faithfully preached? Is it, as some think, that higher criticism is beginning to do its work?

Higher criticism is a method of biblical interpretation that has been used by some to critique the Scriptures from the standpoint of human reasoning, while at the same time discounting the Bible's inerrancy and inspiration. This method has been used for years, but in religious matters, it takes more than a generation for error to work out its evil consequences.

Is it, perhaps, that Christ is preached, that the doctrine is sound, but that the gospel is preached with persuasive words of human wisdom and not in demonstration of the Spirit and power?

Or, is it simply that worldliness and selfishness, along with the pleasure-seeking and money-loving spirit, have so poisoned the whole atmosphere that the Holy Spirit cannot reach through to win young hearts for Christ and His service?

Can it be that churches have a reputation for being alive when they are truly dead (Rev. 3:1)? Is the whole church suffering from a low vitality that is not deep or intense or living enough to attract people to Christ and His service?

There is still another question that leads us deeper into the real condition of things: What does God think of it? When Joshua saw Israel defeated before her enemies, he felt at once that it was a sign that God had withdrawn His presence from His people. And God confirmed this thought: "Israel has sinned ... I will not be with you anymore, unless you destroy whatever among you is devoted to destruction" (Josh. 7:11-12).

The decline in membership has this most solemn aspect – it is a token of God's displeasure. The promise by which the church alone can live, of the power of His Holy Spirit and His grace working with His servants, is not fulfilled. He has turned away His face in grief and great sorrow. That is the meaning of the decline in conversions.

The church may rejoice in what it considers all the tokens of God's favor in the past. However, the lack of conversions and spiritual power is the sure sign that He has withdrawn the real proof of His presence – His saving power in the conversion of sinners. God, who answered Joshua when he fell on his face at the loss of God's presence, will come near to us as we wait for Him, and He will reveal the cause of our defeat.

And now, the last and the crucial question: What is to be done? The years have been allowed to pass by without any definite, full, and final dealing with the question. God waits to hear what we have to say and what we propose to do to put away the evil from us. This must happen before there can be any hope of our restoration to the position of a church in which He can dwell and work mightily for the honor of His name.

In the past, we had such high expectations of an increase in power for carrying on God's work. Yet now, God comes and reveals what little power we have, and how much we are lacking the one thing that Christ longs for and the angels rejoice in – the salvation of souls.

Let us turn to God, each one for himself. Let us ask Him to give us the spiritual insight into the true state of things that we need so much. When you pray, ask Him for the spirit of penitence that has been so lacking. Ask for the spirit of faith, a strong and living faith, that takes hold of Him and will not let Him go until He blesses us.

Allow me to end this chapter with the words of the Reverend C. Bardsley:

How can we impress the mind of the church as a whole? The rank and file of the Christian church needs to grasp the truth that the evangelization of the world is the primary task, the central duty of the church. This will never happen, however, until a more definite lead in a more definite manner is given by the leadership of the church.

How can they give that lead? First, they must be possessed of the truth themselves. They must be obviously full of this truth. They must be absolutely enthusiastic and deadly earnest themselves.

Secondly, they must give opportunities to their people for intercession and praise for foreign missions. How much regular intercession and praise for foreign missions is there in the regular worship of our churches?

Thirdly, if evangelization is indeed the greatest task, it should dominate the gatherings of the church leaders whenever they come together to consider the things of the kingdom of God. There are other matters of importance, but not as important. Let us put first things first when we are gathered together.

You are called ...
To ask God for the Spirit of faith,
a strong and living faith.

CHAPTER 14

Contrition, Confession, Consecration

> He who conceals his sins does not prosper, but who-
> ever confesses and renounces them finds mercy.
>
> – Proverbs 28:13

I have taken the title for this chapter from an article in a missionary magazine. The article gave an account of the powerful working of God's Spirit at a certain revival. In this revival, people who had been Christians for a long time were brought by the Holy Spirit into true brokenness of heart and penitence for sins in their Christian lives.

When the contrition had fully mastered them,

they confessed before both God and man what they had done. Faith that their confession was accepted gave them courage for a new consecration of mingled joy and trembling.

Does this story not teach us a lesson? Where God's children are brought face-to-face with a great evil that has been allowed in the church, His Holy Spirit will work the same deep contrition and penitent confession in answer to prayer. Without this confession, there can be no hope of restoration to full pardon or to true consecration.

The twofold charge against the church, that of neglecting her own members and neglecting the unbelievers entrusted to her, does indeed call for the deepest contrition. Somewhere along the way, there must have been a lack of watchfulness and prayer. There must have been a lack of spiritual life and power in the congregations concerned.

There must have been, on the part of ministers – they will be the first to acknowledge it – a lack of the devotion, faith and prayer that would have faced the evil before it had attained such proportions.

The great thought that we must comprehend is the dishonor and the grief that we have caused God. He has been grieved by the neglect of the lost ones, by the reproach resting on the church of His beloved Son, and by the terrible thwarting of His strong desire to bless the world through the church.

Spiritual truth like this cannot be grasped by the natural mind. It is by God's Spirit alone that it can get full possession of our hearts. What is more, it takes time alone with God in order for Him to breathe and then to deepen the spirit of contrition. It takes turning away from the world and its numberless interests and waiting on God to bow and bend our hearts.

Contrition must become such a reality that we feel something of the pain of a broken heart and offer this sacrifice to God as a felt, living reality. Where such contrition has been worked by the Spirit, He whose name is holy will come to dwell. He will dwell with him who has a contrite and humble heart.

Such contrition must first be found in secret, at least by some who mourn before God for their own state and the state of the church around them. However, then they will desire to help others. The church is a living body; each member cares for and suffers with the others.

The contrite person will find like-minded believers to cultivate and strengthen this spirit of penitence and humility. By the grace of God, the gracious influence will spread. Ministers will begin to properly express God's claims and promises.

Let us ask God with our whole hearts to give the spirit of true, deep, abiding contrition to all who seek it. As we think of all the sins that are implied by this decrease of membership, we will feel the need of the conviction of the Holy Spirit to bring us into the right attitude before God. There are the sins of blood guiltiness, of unfaithfulness in the discharge of our duty, of unbelief in not trusting God for His grace, of negligence in prayer and fellowship with God – all calling for deep humiliation.

After contrition comes confession. There is, I am sorry to say, a religion in which the confession of sin is too easy. People think that it is a matter of course that we sin, and they are sure that, if we only confess, God is ready to pardon.

This is not the confession God's Word speaks of. "Whoever confesses and renounces them [his sins] finds mercy" (Prov. 28:13). That alone is the repentance that does not need to be repented of. As someone has said, "True repentance has restoring power; it never leaves you in the place in which you were."

Confession and forsaking sin make up true contrition, and this is why it is so hard for an honest person to confess his sin. He knows that God expects him to confess and forsake. But where contrition has been deep and true, the Christian will find that it is impossible for him to confess without forsaking.

Sin is very awful and God-dishonoring. It is not a simple or an easy thing to truly confess it. It means a transaction with God in which the sin is brought out, dealt with, and given up to God in the faith that He is righteous to forgive our sins and to cleanse us from all unrighteousness (1 John 1:9). Again, I say, nothing but the deep contrition that the Holy Spirit works can prepare us for true and full confession and forsaking.

Once this has been done in secret before God, then it is time to do it before man, too. However, the order may sometimes be reversed. In a group, under the moving of the Holy Spirit, the confession of one or more may help to rouse others to follow the example. But there is always a danger in this of superficiality. This is safe only if people are led from public confession to the inner chamber of their hearts, not to rest until they know that God has met them and accepted from them the sacrifice of a broken heart.

Everything depends on knowing that there has been a definite transaction between God and the soul. This will give public confession its value and will help stir and strengthen others to follow in the same path.

Above all, full confession is what will give confidence for a full and entire consecration. A group of church leaders had this to say: "God is demanding of us all a new order of life, of a more arduous and self-sacrificing nature than the old." They added that we must "face the new task with a new consecration." Where the contrition and confession that I have spoken of have been full and true, a full and true consecration becomes possible, or rather, becomes a necessity to the penitent heart.

There are various ways of describing the terms of consecration. Keswick has one. Dr. Mott has another. Our godly fathers had their own. They had a deep reverence for God. They knew what it was to give themselves up to His will and to live lives of devoted service and holy fellowship with Him.

There are thousands of Christians who long to be helped to such a life, but they cannot understand how it can come about. May God raise up believers in the pulpit and in the pew who can testify to their fellow believers that Christ can keep strong the soul that trusts Him. He will not only keep him strong, but enable him to walk in His presence all the day!

The church needs to be lifted up out of her feebleness into the abundant life of Christ. But this can happen only if ministers and other believers take a new stand of separation from sin and the world, yielding themselves in a fuller surrender than ever before to follow Christ and live for Him alone. A revival among God's children cannot even be thought of unless the average standard of religion with which we have been content is replaced. This mediocrity must make way, through the power of faith and the Holy Spirit, for a much more tender walk with Christ and a much more complete yielding of our whole beings upon the altar of sacrifice.

Can it be that God is going to do this? Consider the shame and humiliation with which many ministers have looked at the result of their work. Consider the many church members who have confessed their share in the low vitality and feeble spirituality that had so much to do with it. Can it be that God will bring a wonderful blessing out of this? He is most willing to work contrition, accept confession, and strengthen for consecration.

And will He do it? That rests with us. The thought is unspeakably solemn, but the situation is just as solemn. He waits, He longs, He is working to draw His children to Himself. Oh, do not hesitate to bow before Him and listen to His voice:

I want you to know that I am not doing this for your sake, declares the Sovereign LORD. Be ashamed and disgraced for your conduct O house of Israel! (Ezek. 36:32)

Let us not wait for others to begin. If you have experienced any touch of God's Spirit as you have read and thought about the present crisis, if you have had any desire to pray that the mighty power of the Holy Spirit will breathe on the church, begin at once. Plead with God for His almighty grace, and do not rest until you know that, as a contrite penitent, your consecration has been accepted and sealed. Then go out as a living witness to help to bring Christ's call of repentance to the ears of His people. Lead all who will listen to the place of decision and full consecration.

You are called ...

He who conceals his sins does
not prosper, but whoever confesses
and renounces them finds mercy.
— Proverbs 28:13

CHAPTER 15

Repent!

Repent and do the things you did at first. If you do not repent, I will come to you and remove your lamp stand from its place.

— Revelation 2:5

The book of Revelation contains the letters to the seven churches of Asia Minor. In these letters we have a series of pictures of the conditions of several ministers and their people. They have been taken by Him whose eyes are like a flame of fire, searching out and showing forth the actual state of the church.

Out of His mouth goes a sharp sword, for what He sees He speaks of in words of such divine power that they can touch the heart. After the many centuries that have past, these words can still meet the needs of the churches of our day and work in us all that He teaches and commands.

The book of Revelation was written many years after Christ's ascension to heaven. Christ had finished His teaching on earth and had left the further instruction of His disciples to the apostles. Then, after keeping silence for more than half a century, Christ again desired to give some last words to the church on earth. What a solemn thought!

We have these words in the second and third chapters of Revelation. In them, Christ tells us what the smaller portion of the church is like. This part of the church pleases Him. Then He tells us what the majority is like. They are not what they should be. Christ gives the teaching for ministers to use to plead with the majority to return to Him as their Lord.

One of the central words in these letters is the word *repent*. There are only two letters, those to Smyrna and Philadelphia, in which the word *repent* does not appear. Of these two churches the Lord had only good to say. To Smyrna He said, "I know your afflictions and your poverty – yet you are rich! Do not be afraid." (see Rev. 2:9-10.) To Philadelphia He said:

I know that you have little strength, yet you have kept My word and have not denied My name. Since you have kept My command to endure patiently, I will also keep you from the hour of trial. (Rev. 3:8, 10)

I praise God that there are churches on earth in which the majority satisfy the heart of the Son of God!

Then we have the letter to Thyatira, in which the word *repent* occurs, although not as an address to the minister of the church. There was much to be praised: "I know your deeds, your love and faith, your service and perseverance, and that you are now doing more than you did at first" (Rev. 2:19). But there was one evil: the woman Jezebel was allowed to spread her evil influence. God had given her time to repent, but she did not repent.

And then come four churches in which the word *repent* is used in the singular; in other words, it is addressed to the minister as well as the people.

To Ephesus, after mentioning eight things in which they had proved their discipleship, He said, "Yet I hold this against you: You have forsaken your first love" (Rev. 2:4).

In all the highest relationships of life, love is everything. Between a mother and a child, a husband and a wife, a king and his people, love is the chief thing. And so it is between us and Christ. There may be diligence in His service, there may be zeal for the honor of His name, there may be patient endurance of suffering for Him, and yet Christ's heart can be satisfied with nothing less than the first love. This love is the compelling love that delights in His fellowship, yielding itself wholly to His personal influence and giving a living testimony about Him.

Amid all the activities of the church at Ephesus, true, tender love for Christ was lacking. It is about this that Christ said, "Remember the height from which you have fallen! Repent and do the things you did at first" (Rev. 2:5). As we think of the failure of the church of our day in regard to making Christ known and her utter unfitness for taking up the work to which she is now being led, do we not here find the secret cause of it all, the lack of personal love for Christ?

And does not the word of the Lord come to us, too, "If you do not repent, I will come to you and remove your lamp stand from its place" (v. 5)?

To Pergamum He said, "I have a few things against you" (v. 14). Their sin was that they tolerated false teachers. His word to them was, "Repent" (v. 16).

It is often said that higher criticism and its advanced teaching has much to do with the loss of power in our preaching and the lack of an earnest Christian life among believers. In chapter four I quoted a writer who said, "In many of our churches the great underlying doctrines and facts of the gospel are scarcely ever referred to in preaching." He went on to say, "A personal appeal to the conscience and a direct effort for conversion are seldom witnessed."

I have heard more than one public testimony regarding the lack of the full and fearless preaching of Christ and His Cross. Even those who are sound in doctrine themselves are still too silent in regard to exposing preaching that they know cannot satisfy the church's need or exercise divine power to salvation.

Christ's command to repent is a call to us to evaluate whether our teaching is truly the proclamation of the message of God's inspired Word, or whether it seeks to please men by its excellency of speech and persuasive words of human wisdom.

To Sardis He said, "I know your deeds; you have a reputation of being alive, but you are dead" (Rev. 3:1). He then said, in essence, "I have found no works of yours completed before My God. Remember how you have received, and repent."

In Dr. Denney's address, from which I have already quoted, he spoke of many people who are "lovers of pleasures rather than lovers of God" (2 Tim. 3:4). They refuse to give up anything for Christ's sake. I will repeat his words here, "I say the world is full of people like that, and what is worse, whoever is to blame for it, the church is full of them, too. As far as these people are concerned, the Christian religion is dead."

What an awful description – a church full of such people! And it was of this condition that Christ said, "You have a reputation of being alive, but you are dead" (Rev. 3:1). It is to such a church today that Christ's first word is "repent" (v. 3).

To Laodicea He said:

> I know your deeds, that you are neither cold nor hot. I wish you were either one or the other! You say, "I am rich; I have acquired wealth and do not need a thing." But you do not realize that you are wretched, pitiful, poor, blind and naked. (Rev. 3:15, 17)

Do we not have here a true picture of a great many of our churches and our Christians – neither cold nor hot, but lukewarm, with a "form of godliness but denying its power" (2 Tim. 3:5), seeking and succeeding according to their own minds, uniting the friendship of God with the friendship of the world?

As the result of this, the spirit of self-satisfaction and mutual self-congratulation is heard everywhere, with its deep undertone, "[We are] rich, and have everything, and do not need anything." And Christ answers solemnly, "You do not realize that you are lost."

How does Christ deal with these lukewarm, self-satisfied Christians? He has, again, just that same solemn word for them, "Repent" (Rev. 3:19). Whatever the evil is, there is but one gate out of it – that hard, stern, but blessed word, "*repent*."

Just think for a moment of the four churches that have been mentioned.

In Ephesus, the problem was a lack of love. Compelling love for Christ was no longer found.

In Pergamum, it was a lack of truth. They had forsaken the inspired Word. They tolerated the teaching of error.

In Sardis, the problem was a lack of life. They had a reputation that they were alive, but they were actually dead.

In Laodicea, it was a lack of fire. The baptism of the Spirit and of fire was no longer known.

Whatever the sin of a church may be, however closely the minister and people may be bound together in sin, Christ in heaven has one message, "Repent."

Think of what that means, coming from Him who gave His life to win our hearts for Himself. He is now seated on the throne in order to give repentance. He pleads with us by His cross and His blood. He seeks to touch the heart and break it with that love of His.

With a voice of infinite holiness and tenderest compassion, He pleads with those whom His heart-searching words have warned and roused – just that one word, "Repent."

This is the word that He commissions the ministers of the churches to sound in the ears of His people, to bring near and to open up to them, to plead with them until they bow before it, "Repent."

He spoke the word, first of all, to the minister of the church himself. Whether he had been found lacking in love for Christ or in the truth of Christ or in the life of Christ or in the fire of Christ, He called him to repentantly come and receive His pardon and the new experience of His blessing and power. He then sent him forth to sound out with his whole heart the note of warning and of welcome, "Repent, oh, my people, repent."

We are accustomed to using the word *repent* in our missionary work or in our ordinary evangelistic preaching. However, the ministers to whom Christ has committed the oversight of the churches – and the decline of membership proves what a lack of power there has been in their preaching and spiritual lives – are called to take up the word *repent* in its deeper meaning.

The church of Christ is on the decline. In the seven churches of Revelation, we have examples of the various stages of spiritual decline in our churches today, and their implications.

In the Ephesus stage, the defection begins with the loss of the first love, even amid great zeal for the truth. In the Pergamum stage, we discover a step lower: God's holy Word is no longer taken as the only standard of teaching. In the Sardis stage, the evil becomes still more manifest: with a reputation for being alive, the church is dead.

In the Laodicea stage, it reaches its full growth: people are so utterly unconscious of anything wrong, so satisfied with themselves and with each other, so blind to what Christ calls their wretchedness and nakedness, that they proudly boast in their meetings and reports: "I am rich; I have acquired wealth and do not need a thing" (Rev. 3:17).

What a work it is for the ministers of the churches to take that word *repent* from Christ's own lips while on their knees, to bow to it with their whole hearts, and then in the power of His Spirit to carry it throughout the church as the one great means of revival and restoration!

Let no one think, "This message is too hard. Who can bear it?" Listen to what Christ says of it:

"Those whom I love I rebuke and discipline. So be

earnest, and repent. Here I am! I stand at the door and knock. If anyone hears My voice and opens the door, I will come in and eat with him, and he with Me." (Rev. 3:19-20)

Do not be afraid, O minister of God, to sound the word *repent* loud and clear. It is Christ's infinite love that speaks the word, that will give the blessing with it, that will reveal Himself to His penitent people. Out of the fullness of a living faith in the love of Christ, call believers to repent in the assurance of His welcome and His blessing. Christ closes each of these seven letters with these words: "He who has an ear, let him hear what the Spirit says to the churches" (Rev. 2:7). Let the minister of Christ take these words into the depth of his heart. Let him pray and believe until he is sure the blessed Spirit is speaking through him. Let him tell the church that the power of the Spirit is working to reveal Christ and His love. And let him from this point forward carry on His work as never before.

Let him be assured that, in answer to much prayer, the mighty power of the Spirit will secretly work and will restore God's children in the path of repentance to a new and more abundant life. Then, there will no longer be any reason to complain of the decline in membership or of a lack of loyalty to Christ and His service.

CHAPTER 16

The Valley of Decision

Multitudes, multitudes in the valley of decision! For the day of the LORD is near in the valley of decision.

– Joel 3:14

These questions are often asked by believers: "What is it about certain Christian meetings that so influences people? What brings the power that is not felt in the ordinary services of the same speaker?" The answers are found in the fact that people are invited to come to the meetings with a definite need. Then they are helped toward a definite step for the fulfillment of that need.

Is this not the great secret of the success of our evangelists? They occupy people intensely and continually with the thought of their need of salvation and the possibility of their obtaining it at once. It is the same way in conferences on the spiritual life. People who feel burdened by the thought of their continual sinning and their powerlessness in seeking victory are invited to come and hear how deliverance can be obtained. The speaker's emphasis on making the right decision is the key. By this, he influences people to do and to be what they ought.

The same secret of success in preaching the gospel can be found in other spheres. All who have heard Dr. John Mott know how the emphasis is placed on immediate decision. Years ago, Dr. Mott did a remarkable work among the students of Edinburgh.

In his whole appeal to the will, the students were made to feel a contagious influence that gave them courage to hope for deliverance. His was not a teaching that people were to take home and think about. Some may have done so, but with most of them, help was found in Dr. Mott's confident emphasis on the real possibility of a present and immediate change.

This was the same emphasis that ran through all his work among Christian students. He pleaded for an irrevocable surrender to the vow of spending at least half an hour every morning with God. This caused many to give up habits of laziness and self-indulgence and, as a result, to consecrate the whole day to the service of God. It was on this account that he so often used the following words, both in speaking and writing:

Next to the act of conversion, in which a man turns from sin to God, and after that, of the reception of the Holy Spirit as the power of a new life, I know of nothing that will aid a man so much in the Christian life as the undiscouragable resolution to spend at least half an hour in the morning alone with God.

The apparently simple act of the will in making the decision meant nothing less than a full surrender to live for God and His will.

It was that same call for decision that appealed so mightily and successfully for volunteers for the foreign mission field. This truth was underscored: Christ's command to preach the gospel to every individual is a command to every disciple. The preacher preached this with all the urgency of a man who himself had yielded his whole being to Christ's service. Then an appeal was made to all who were truly willing to show their full allegiance to Christ. They were challenged to say whether there was any reason that they should not accept His call at once.

In *The Life of Douglas Thornton*, we read how he and a friend went out after a meeting into a field under the open heavens in perfect agony about this burden that was being laid on them. They did not rest until they had the courage to make a full surrender.

In the same book, we get a glimpse of the activities of Thornton and other totally committed men during a missionary conference in Liverpool. They threw themselves into the work of prayer and influencing others.

Under the deep conviction that they had actually given themselves to Christ to receive in prayer His guidance and power, they proved what it meant to live wholly for the kingdom.

Dr. Mott has said that the book that has influenced him most in his life is John Foster's *Decision of Character*. The word *decision* is characteristic of his whole work and of that of his fellow workers in the great volunteer movement.

George Sherwood Eddy was a missionary and a delegate to the World Missionary Conference. He gave his testimony concerning the secret of his power:

I remember fifteen years ago, before going to India, sitting down with my roommate, now in China, and saying to him, "What are we going to tell them out there on the field? What message have we got for people? Are we merely going to tell them about Christ? If so, it would be cheaper to send out Bibles and tracts. Can we tell them that we know Jesus Christ saves and satisfies, that He keeps us more than conquerors day by day.

I went on to say, "I am not satisfied. I do not feel that I have a message such as I need for people out there, or the experience, or the power. If we do not have these, do you not agree that the one great thing we need before we leave this country is to know Him?"

From that day to the end of our student days, we rose every morning at five o'clock. From five to six we had an unhurried hour for the Word of God, and from six to seven an unhurried hour for prayer. These two hours each day changed our lives, and we were unspeakably blessed.

That valley of decision was to them truly the valley of blessing. And God has set His seal to it in the fruit of Mr. Eddy's work.

It is this note of decision that is too often lacking in our evangelical preaching. It is this note that will be greatly needed if slumbering or weak, but well-meaning Christians are truly to be roused.

People are content when they hear what they think is a profitable message. They carry away the impression that the message has made on them, and they hope that in some way or other an effect will be produced. And still they go on in that halfhearted religion, which they confess is wrong but which they cannot find the power to reject.

If God's Spirit begins to truly move in the church, the preaching will need an emphasis on decision that we have little known. The hearer must feel that he is called to face a crisis. He is to say whether or not he is really going to yield to Christ's claim and surrender his heart and life to His service. By the grace of God, the minister must seek to get hold of the hearer and not let him go until the decision is made.

Why have I written all this? I feel deeply that unless a call for believers to immediately repent is sounded throughout the church, unless they are reassured that they can be restored to a life of devotion to Christ, there is no prospect of a true response to Christ's claim.

The passages in chapter two about the power-lessness of the church and the disloyalty of Christians to their Savior ring in my ears.

How I wish that every thoughtful, prayerful friend of missions could embrace these words and devote himself to comprehending their full meaning.

Surely the questions would then come with tremendous urgency: "Can anything be done to bring Christians to a sense of their shame? Can they be brought to desire the restoration of that spirit of loyalty and devotion without which Christianity is just a form?"

Are we to look to the ministers to lead people to a conviction of what is wrong in their Christian lives, to a desire for what is better, to a faith in the possibility of an entire change in all who are willing to receive it? If so, we must have ministers in whom the Spirit of God works a faith in the power of Christ, a faith that will enable them to inspire their hearers with an entirely new hope.

And where are these ministers to be found? Surely there must be many whose hearts burn with the passion of Jesus Christ for mankind. But many are not conscious of the power God can exert through them. If they truly come to know the power of Jesus Christ to keep them loyal and true, they will have a message that will certainly reach some hearts.

Let loyalty to Christ – full, unflinching, whole-hearted loyalty – become the keynote of their praying and their preaching. Let a few band themselves together to ask God for this one full insight into the terrible condition of a church in which so few members are won to Christ by the preaching of the Word.

Let them offer themselves to God for a new

baptism of His Spirit and a new power to preach about the Day of the Lord and about His presence in the midst of His people.

Let them not rest until they begin to gather together, however few they may be, souls who are willing to be living witnesses that Jesus Christ does indeed save from the power of selfishness and the world. He does indeed enable ordinary men and women to live with His life so much in their hearts that the conquest of the world for Him is the greatest reality, the all-absorbing purpose of their life and their love.

Teachers of psychology and ethics tell us that the first step in breaking the power of an old habit or in cultivating an entirely new one is to take the initiative with full purpose of heart.

Everything should be done, by pledge or public confession, to break away at once from the old and to commit oneself with no room for compromise. They say that the application of this principle will give, in many cases, the needed help to those who otherwise despair of deliverance.

This plan is just what is needed by the preacher who comes to call weak, sluggish Christians to a new life of loyalty and devotion.

If believers can be brought to confess the error of their position, and their powerlessness to make it right, to believe that Christ by His Spirit can strengthen them to escape from the bondage in which they have been serving self and the world, they will find the courage to take the decisive step.

Faith that Christ is able to keep them in a close relationship with Himself, which makes a life of consecration possible and most blessed, will enable them to step out in full surrender to His mighty power. The church will see what wonders God can do in those who wait on Him.

Let us simply have witnesses, in the pulpit or out of it, in whom the power of a living testimony sounds the notes of victory. Then we will find that God is faithful to give revival where otherwise all had been hopeless.

It is in the valley of decision that such preachers and such witnesses are found. It is in the valley of decision, that is, the valley of judgment, that a man feels utterly condemned and yet takes courage to believe in what Christ can make of him. There the church will find the secret of her lost power. She will find courage for a surrender to Christ and His service that seeks to know of no other standard than that of the love in which He gave Himself for us.

"Multitudes, multitudes in the valley of decision" (Joel 3:14). That will be the prayer of many. But, please understand that we may not wait until multitudes are there.

Let each one who hears the call of God go down, even if he is all alone, into the valley of decision, and yield himself as a willing sacrifice into His hands.

You are called ...

To make a decision today to yield yourself anew to Christ.

CHAPTER 17

The Ministry

If you remain in Me and My words remain in you,
ask whatever you wish, and it will be given to you.

– John 15:7

I feel that I have come to the most important and the most difficult chapter of my book. I cannot help thinking that a special appeal to the ministers would rouse much thought and prayer. Under a deep sense of my insufficiency for the task of speaking to my fellow preachers, I will try to express the message that this book brings to the minister.

The first thought is the heavy responsibility that rests on the minister. We have been reading of the failure of the church and of the low state of spiritual life that is the cause of her failure. All this is, first of all, an appeal to the ministry. It comes with the question, "Why is it that things are in such poor shape, and what is to be done to remedy the situation?"

Many church leaders lay the responsibility on the ministry. Take a look at the following thoughts:

As far as the interest of the church in missions is concerned, the minister holds the key to the situation.

In the work of the ministers is found the secret of the real condition existing in the church.

Invariably, a missionary pastor makes a missionary church.

There is no doubt that in order to arouse the church to a sense of its opportunity and privilege, the clergy must be reached and their enthusiastic cooperation secured.

On ministers, more than on all others, falls the duty of educating the church about its missionary calling and of supplying the people with the enthusiasm that will make the church equal in spiritual power to the present world situation.

Are we prepared to admit and accept this tremendous responsibility? Will we confess our share in the church's failure and yield ourselves, by the grace of God, at every sacrifice, to fulfill our task?

How is it possible that the majority of ministers have never realized what their duty is, or, when it was put before them, did not have the power and the courage to fulfill it?

In answer to that question, we are reminded that the church as a whole must share the blame. She has never, through her theological colleges, trained her young students to fulfill this part of their high calling.

Yes, she has tried to encourage ministers and members who are interested in missionary work to exercise all their influence.

However, she has never clearly and strongly declared the truth that every minister and every member is to live and labor so that Christ may be made known to every living individual. These colleges have not trained ministers to carry out this task.

However, this explanation does not relieve us from the responsibility that God has put on us, and which He would have taught us, had we known what it is to live in continual prayer for His teaching.

This is another great defect of our theological

training: how little we were taught that, in the true ministry, prayer is the first and most essential thing. It was not that our professors did not sometimes remind us of the need for prayer, but it was taken for granted that we knew how to pray and did pray.

Not long ago, I was told about two ministers who were talking on the subject, mourning that in their college training they had not been taught to acquire the secret of prayer. One said, "It is not that the subject was not mentioned, but it was not impressed upon us that prayer is the first secret of success in the ministry." The patterns of student life are naturally carried forward into the ministry, and we find it so hard to acquire the habit of truly effective prayer amid all the study and work that occupies our time.

Yet, it is just in this matter of prayer that the responsibility lies on us so heavily. If we are to do our part, if we are to train our people to yield themselves to Christ's claim, we must, above all, learn to pray.

How to multiply the number of Christians who with clear, unshakable faith in the character of God will wield this force of intercession – that is the supreme question of foreign missions. Every other consideration is secondary to that of wielding the forces of prayer.

The primary need is not the multiplication of prayer meetings, but that individual Christians should learn to pray … Every endeavor must be made to spread the spirit and habit of prayer among all Christian workers.

What a responsibility rests on the minister in the matter of his own intercession and in the training of God's people to take part in it!

I have spoken of the lack in our training, as theological students, of enthusiasm for missions and the power of intercession. I feel that I must mention something that goes still deeper.

You have read more than once in this book that the lack of interest in missions and of devotion in prayer can be traced to the feeble vitality, to the low spiritual life prevailing in the church. And it is just this that many ministers never learn at college: that the power to pray, and the power to teach others to pray, is entirely dependent on the depth of one's spiritual life.

Did our Lord Jesus not say, "If you remain in Me and My words remain in you, ask whatever you wish, and it will be given to you" (John 15:7)? Many a believer has resolved to pray more, but has failed, because he did not know this secret, that the average Christian life is not sufficient to provide power with God in prayer.

It requires self-denial, a turning away from the world, and the sacrifice of what may appear legitimate to others. A heart that is given up to God and longs to be led by the Holy Spirit is needed if one is to claim all the wonderful promises in God's Word connected with prayer.

Listen once again to a passage from a church leader:

> The superhuman must be emphasized as never before since the days of the early church. Christians need a fuller, more constant, and more commanding realization of the personal presence of Christ.

That means there must be the experience of a closer daily fellowship with Him than is ordinarily thought possible. Read these two reminders:

> Conferences have been held where the work of world evangelization has received careful consideration, but there has been alarming neglect in facing the great central problem, namely, how to translate into actual experience these words of Christ: "If a man remains in Me and I in him, he will bear much fruit; apart from Me you can do nothing" (John 15:5).
>
> The missionary problem of the church today is not primarily a financial problem. The problem is how to ensure a vitality equal to the ex-

pansion of the missionary program. The only hope of this is for Christians to obtain the more abundant life through Christ.

Everything returns to this question: Does the church have sufficient vitality for the tremendous task to which it is called? That sufficient vitality is what the ministers need first of all if they are to lead the church to it. On the ministers rests the responsibility of lifting the church up out of her feeble vitality into the abundant life that there is in Christ Jesus.

What a responsibility! "Who is equal to such a task?" (2 Cor. 2:16). "Our competence comes from God. He has made us competent as ministers ... of the Spirit" (2 Cor. 3:5-6).

God never lays responsibility on His servant without the assurance of sufficient grace for all that He expects him to be.

Let this thought turn the sense of responsibility into prayer. And let all that we have learned about the absolute necessity and the limitless possibilities of prayer just lead us to cast ourselves upon God, in the confidence that He will equip us for the place that we are being called upon to take in the world conquest.

You remember the instance I gave in chapter sixteen, "The Valley of Decision," of the decision of two young students to give an hour each day to prayer. What do you think? Would it be too much for you to ask God for grace to spend half an hour, every day, in addition to your ordinary time, just to learn from Him the art of prayer and intercession?

In that school you will get the necessary training for that power of prayer that will lead you into the abundant life of Christ as never before. Then you will be ready for the great work of lifting up the church into the same place of power and blessing.

With faith in God's promise, do not be afraid, but go down into the valley of decision. Let it be your firm resolve to spend that half hour with God in special prayer for your own need and the need of His church concerning the new consecration to the service of His kingdom. By the grace of God, the decision for that half hour may be a decision for a life of new devotion to God and His will.

The hesitation and self-reproach for unfaithfulness in the morning brings, unconsciously, a cloud all day. The decision to do God's will at any cost in the morning hour casts us upon Christ and makes the will strong for the whole day. And the decision for the day may give us courage for the next day, and lead us on to a walk with God day by day.

What a responsibility rests on the ministers

in this question of the feeble spiritual life of the church and in their commitment to pray to God to lift her out of her low state into the sunlight of His love.

You are called ...

To live in continual prayer.

CHAPTER 18

A Plea for More Prayer

I will do whatever you ask in My name, so that the Son may bring glory to the Father.

– John 14:13

What a difference there is between the first mountain springs where a great river has its origin and the vast expanse of water where it reaches the sea and carries fleets of ships on its surface.

Such, and even much greater, is the difference between prayer in the simplicity of its first beginnings and the incomprehensible mystery of what it becomes when it makes man a partner with God in the rule of the world. Instead of being the simple channel through which a child or a new convert obtains his request from God, it becomes the heavenly power that can channel all the riches of God and bring down the blessings of the Spirit on countless souls.

What a study prayer is! I do not know whether to thank God most for prayer in its blessed simplicity, in which it is the comfort of those who hardly ever go beyond their personal needs, or in its profound depths, in which it reveals to us how close and wonderful the union is between God and man.

I feel that I cannot end this book without once again attempting to point you to this latter aspect of it. I do so with fear and trembling. The thoughts are so wonderful and beyond our reach that I hardly venture to hope that I can make them plain. Yet, with God's help, I must make the attempt.

When God undertook the work of creating man after His own likeness, His great purpose was to have a being in whom He could perfectly reveal all the glory of His divine power. Man was to be here on earth what God is in heaven, the king and ruler. He was made in the image of God in this especially, that just as God is self-determined and is what He is by His own blessed will, so man also, as far as a creature dependent on God could do so, was to fashion his own character and being. Man was to prepare himself for the power of ruling others.

As we are told in Revelation 1:6, we have been made "a kingdom and priests." As priests, we turn our face Godward to worship and receive His blessing. As kings, we turn manward to dispense that blessing in ruling and guiding others.

The great thought of God was to train man for the place that he is to have with Christ upon the throne. God's purpose was that man should rule in such a way that God would do nothing except through him, and that man should understand that he would do nothing except through God.

It is in this wonderful relationship that prayer has its mystery and its glory. God promises to give His Spirit and to exercise His power according to the will of man (when, of course, it is aligned with God's will).

If man will avail himself of his high prerogative and fully yield himself to the Holy Spirit's teaching in regard to the will of God, God will make literally true what Christ promised: "If you remain in Me and My words remain in you, ask whatever you wish, and it will be given you" (John 15:7). The prayer of faith will move mountains.

We are told that every aspect of nature seeks to clothe itself in a suitable body. The life in a tree creates for itself, in the fruit, the embodiment of its inmost nature. So it is with God, who is Spirit. The creation of man was not an afterthought, but part of His eternal purpose to reveal Himself completely throughout all creation.

The first step in that path was the creation of man out of the dust, in God's image and likeness. The next was the coming of the eternal Son to unite and forever identify Himself with human nature. Then followed Christ's resurrection from the dead and His ascension to heaven in His glorified humanity. And last of all came the outpouring of the Holy Spirit, by which the church became, "His body, the fullness of Him who fills everything in every way" (Eph. 1:23). In that body Christ is to be revealed when He comes in glory, and in that body the Father will dwell in the Son. Throughout all eternity, man is to be the revelation of what God is, and through man Christ will rule the world.

It is in prayer that man takes his part even now in the rule of the world. As a preparation for his future glory, he, even now, in the holy priesthood of intercession, begins to understand what the inconceivable power of prayer can be. Prayer is the highest proof of the image of God in which we have been created. Prayer is the exercise of our king-like privilege of ruling the world.

The point at which it becomes difficult for us to believe all this is when we are told that God is longing to pour out blessing, but is prevented from doing so by His people. They are the hindrance. God allows His work to suffer loss, terrible loss, because He will not break the law He Himself made. He respects the liberty He Himself gave man. In infinite long-suffering, He bides His time until man becomes willing to pray and receive His blessing.

Let me repeat a thought from a previous chapter:

> We must make believers understand that it is only their halfhearted consecration and lack of faith that hinder the rapid advance of the work, only their own coldness that keeps back His redemption from a lost world. We must always bear in mind that He is eager and able to save the world, which has already been redeemed by Him. Alas, if only we, His professed followers on earth, were willing that He do so.

One would think that on hearing this people would say, "It is impossible. It cannot be true that millions are perishing because God's people are not praying." But it is true. However, it is a truth that the natural mind cannot grasp. It is only the Holy Spirit who can enlighten the heart to comprehend the spiritual reality of this wonderful partnership between God and His people in the salvation of the world.

One would ask, "How can the church be so foolish as to spend all her strength in doing a work that is comparatively a failure, that ends in a decline of membership, when she has the divine promise that in answer to prayer the power of the Holy Spirit can make the dry bones live?" There is no explanation but this: People hear the promise with the hearing of the ear, but the truth has no power over them. They simply do not yield themselves, in holy fellowship with God, to receive the Spirit and the Spirit-born conviction that prayer can bring down into their hearts the life that there is in Christ Jesus.

How often the complaint is heard that it is so hard to pray properly, to pray enough, to pray in power. The reason is simple: We think of prayer mainly as a means of getting blessing for ourselves. We think very little about yielding ourselves entirely to holy fellowship with God and to the self-denying sacrifice needed in bearing the needs of others.

We are hardly conscious of the fact that we are kings. No wonder we have so little confidence in our priestly access to God for the work of bringing down blessing on the world. A man's thoughts rule his actions; the ideas he fosters make his character. Oh, that God's children might take hold of the wonderful promise that whatsoever they ask in the name of Jesus, it will be done for them (John 14:13). Oh, that they would learn to look upon themselves as God's chosen intercessors, the channels without whom His love cannot do its work. They may be sure that prayer will begin to have a new attraction and that fellowship with God will become their highest privilege.

I fear wearying my reader by the repetition of the chief thoughts of this book. Yet, these ideas are a plea for more prayer. Therefore, I will risk summing up once again what I think God wants us to consider:

- ꙮ The verdict of church leaders that the church is unwilling and unfit for doing the work God puts before her.
- ꙮ The confession of the churches that they are powerless to keep hold of their members because the spirit of the world is too strong.
- ꙮ The sad truth that both of these things are due to a lack of that spiritual life and power without which our work is in vain.
- ꙮ The conviction that nothing but the power of God's Holy Spirit in our hearts and lives can cure the evil.
- ꙮ The belief that God longs with all His heart to give His Spirit to the righteous person whose fervent prayer accomplishes much, so that He may lift His church to the life that she can have in Christ Jesus.

As we study and pray over these thoughts, step by step, in God's presence, the mystery of prayer will open up to us. We will see that God has actually made us partners in the business, has made us kings and priests to dispense His blessings to a feeble church and a perishing world.

We will hear a call to forsake that halfhearted, selfish, prayerless life in which we have lived, and to begin as intercessors to take our place before God. He assures us that He has put the renewal of the church into our hands, and that He will give to persevering, believing intercession the high honor of restoring His children to the life that He meant for them.

Let each of us take a prayer card and write on it the five points I have just mentioned. Let us think and pray over them until we realize that there is really something that needs to be prayed for. Let our hearts get so interested in the need that prayer becomes the spontaneous expression of our strong desire for God's blessing on His church.

You are called ...

To be a channel through which God's love flows.

CHAPTER 19

Fear Not, Only Believe

Don't be afraid; just believe.

– Mark 5:36

Some people possess an easy optimism that they imagine to be faith in God. They think their easy optimism gives them the right and ability to claim every promise in God's Word. They do not understand how inseparably the words *repent* and *believe* are bound together. They have never learned that throughout Scripture a chief element in faith in God is a sense of powerlessness and utter helplessness.

As we near the end of this book, we need to speak about faith. We must give faith its place if we are to go forward with the certain hope that

God's mighty power will be manifested in our own lives, in the church around us, and especially in our ministers. I am speaking of the power manifested as God works in us that deep, intense, living vitality that we are longing for.

In order to apply to ourselves Christ's words, "Don't be afraid, just believe" (Mark 5:36), we must carefully note the attitude of the man to whom they were first given.

We find that Jairus was greatly troubled. His little daughter was at the point of death. He had fallen at Christ's feet and earnestly pleaded with Him to come and lay His hand on her. Jesus went with him. But all at once there was an interruption – a woman touched the hem of Christ's garment – and Jairus feared that they may be too late. His worst fears were realized when messengers came to say, "Your daughter is dead: why bother the Teacher any more?" (Mark 5:35).

It was to this deeply distressed man, who had intensely implored Christ to come and was now brought to utter hopelessness by the news of his daughter's death, that He spoke the words, "Don't be afraid, only believe." The soil had been broken up deeply. The heart was prepared to believe. Christ's precious word entered in and took possession.

Some of us are bearing the burden of a dead or a dying church. If we are going to take part in the work of rousing her and lifting her up into the abundant life that there is in Christ, we need nothing as much as a word like this. It will bring us the joyous assurance day by day that Christ is with us, that He will work through us, and that we can count on Him to give the blessing.

However, we must take the place that Jairus did, falling at His feet, greatly imploring Him to graciously and mightily intervene. Even when the news comes, "There is no hope, death reigns, all our efforts are in vain," we must still take courage and hold on to His Word. "Don't be afraid, only believe" must be our motto.

But it applies only – I say it once again – to the person who waits at Christ's feet in prayer and looks to Him alone. There we will learn that throughout all Scripture it is faith in the midst of seeming impossibility that waits and claims the fulfillment of the promise.

Think of Abraham, who "was strengthened in his faith and gave glory to God ... being fully persuaded that God had power to do what He had promised" (Rom. 4:20-21). As we persevere in prayer, take hold of definite promises, and earnestly appeal to Him to fulfill them, we will hold fast our confidence to the end through every obstacle.

We may find that as time goes on, as our insight into the deadly state of the church grows deeper, and as experience teaches us how very hard it is to rouse Christians to the full meaning of, and surrender to the claims of Christ, our hearts will often grow faint and fail us for fear. Yet, if we have made our covenant with Christ that we dare not go back, but are determined to hold on, we will find that just one word from our Lord, hidden in the heart and lived on day by day, will give strength in the time of greatest darkness.

Just think of the words of Christ in regard to what appears to man to be impossible. He had said of the young ruler, "How hard is it to enter into the kingdom of God!" (Mark 10:24). The disciples had asked, "Who then can be saved?" (v. 26). Christ's answer was, "With man this is impossible," but He added, "All things are possible with God" (v. 27). And He said to the father of the demon-possessed child, "Everything is possible for him who believes" (Mark 9:23). These three sentences – "With man this is impossible," "All things are possible with God," and "Everything is possible for him who believes" – are a cord of three strands that cannot quickly be broken (Eccl. 4:12).

Impossible with Man

First, "With man this is impossible." It seems

easy to say, and yet how difficult it is to realize it and act it out. What is it that hinders the church in this day from falling on its knees and pleading with God by His Holy Spirit to give revival? Nothing but this: People do not consider that the work that they must do is impossible for man. They consult, organize, and labor very diligently, and yet the members decline by the thousands. They cannot see that the work of winning people to become members of Christ and His church is a work that God alone can do through believers who have yielded themselves to the Holy Spirit. What a day it would be if the church were to fall down before God and bow in the dust with the cry, "O God, this is impossible with man."

Possible with God

We should then be prepared for the second lesson: "All things are possible with God" (Mark 10:27). At first sight this appears easy to accept. We are sure that there is nothing impossible with such a God. Yet, when we ask whether God's servants really believe it, whether they wait on Him and expect His working with joyful confidence, we soon find out that they do not. How hard it is to get a deep impression of God's power and of His readiness to work out in us what He has called us to do. God is so little of a reality to us.

How few take time with God so that the blessed sense of His holy presence can fill their hearts and strengthen them in their work.

If you are beginning to take the state of the church to heart, and to bear it as a burden before the Lord, do not be surprised if you have found this difficult to. If you want to fully grasp the truth, "All things are possible with God" (Mark 10:27), in regard to the objects of your work and prayer, learn the lesson of bringing that blessed truth into contact with your daily work and prayer. Let its light shine into your heart, on your sphere of labor, on the church around you, and on the feeblest and most hopeless part of the church, until all your thoughts have this as their keynote: "All things are possible with God" (v. 27). He is able to rouse the church out of her apathy and lift Christians into the abundant life.

He Who Believes

Now comes the third and most difficult lesson: "Everything is possible for him who believes" (Mark 9:23). It is something great to really believe that all things are possible with God, yet the soul may be troubled as to how and when that belief may come. This word of Christ throws the responsibility on us. It is to him who believes that God makes all things possible.

When Christ spoke that word to the father of the demon-possessed child, the man felt his responsibility so deeply, was so concerned that he might lack the necessary faith, that he cried out, "I do believe; help me overcome my unbelief" (Mark 9:24). And Christ heard that prayer.

Our hearts may shrink back with the thought, "Is it going to depend on me whether this mighty God will do the impossible thing? I do not dare to bear the burden of this responsibility." But He is still waiting to strengthen our faith. Jesus Christ, the One who helped the father of the demon-possessed child, who said to Peter, "I have prayed for you, that your faith may not fail" (Luke 22:32), who became man to bring us into fellowship with the omnipotent God, will give us the confidence to believe God. Jesus says, "If you remain in Me and My words remain in you, ask whatever you wish, and it will be given you" (John 15:7). Let us live in fellowship with the One who spoke these words. He will enable us to receive them until they become the joy and the strength of our hearts.

If this book has not established the church's great need of the Holy Spirit and His power, I have failed to fulfill my purpose. But I would fail even more if I were to part from you, without having helped you to this confident assurance: God is able and willing to work revival in answer to prayer and to fill the hearts of His children with a measure of the Holy Spirit that they have never known. As we look out upon a church that is feeble and faithless, let us listen to the voice of Jesus as He says, "Don't be afraid, only believe."

What I have already said, I repeat here. The church around you may be in a dying state, with no possibility of being reached by human effort. I plead with you, look up to God. Wait before Him in prayer until stronger desire is stirred and faith rises to link itself to His omnipotence. Believe in the power of our Lord Jesus and in His tender relationship to you, as He watches over your faith. Believe in the power of the Holy Spirit, which is the promise of the Father and the birthright of the church. His power is surrounding you on every side and longing to take possession of you and those for whom you are praying. Let your review of the state of the church give you a knowledge of God and a trust in Him, beyond what you have ever known or thought.

You are called ...

To take hold of God's promises because He will fulfil them. Believe in Christ's power.

CHAPTER 20

A Personal Word

Love the Lord your God with all your heart and with all your soul and with all your mind and with all your strength.

– Mark 12:30

As we reach the close of this book, I would like to ask what you think of the great problem the church is facing.

This problem may be summarized in these words, which I quoted in chapter one: "The Christian experience of the church is not deep, intense, and living enough to meet the world's need." Also, in previous chapters of this book, I have given other quotations from various leaders, which emphasize the thought that the church lacks the vitality and devotion needed for the tremendous task to which it is called. The all-important question is this: How can the church be lifted up into a fuller spiritual life?

I boldly plead with you to ponder the question until you realize its tremendous solemnity and resolve that you will at least yield yourself as a living sacrifice for God to use for that great work. I ask every child of God to carefully consider the following thoughts.

Will you not take the time and thought and prayer to fully sense the terrible situation? Millions of people are still without the knowledge of Christ. The church has been created, set apart, and clothed with the Spirit for the one purpose of making Christ known to every human being without delay. But the great majority of Christians are utterly indifferent to this. A considerable number are apparently willing to help, but they are utterly unconscious of the urgency of the need or the solemn responsibility resting on them. Only a small number are seeking to yield themselves to fulfill their Lord's command at any cost.

God in heaven holds His omnipotence at the disposal of the faith and prayer of His people, but He is hindered by their unbelief. And Christ the Lord is grieved, oh, so grieved, because His love is so little known and honored by His people, and so little made known to those whom He longs to reach.

I ask you, will you not turn aside from the world and from people to take up this burden of the Lord? Will you wait on God to see if He will use you to help His church to some proper sense of shame and repentance for all this sinful neglect? I know no other way of restoration than for individual men and women to begin by pleading with God on behalf of the church, and by pleading with men on behalf of God. I plead with you, pointedly and personally, will you be one?

You may feel as if you do not have the enthusiasm or the faith for such an undertaking. You are not conscious that you have power with God as an intercessor. You fear that you may not be faithful in fulfilling your vow or in attaining that more abundant life to which you are asked to help lift the church.

I beg you, do not give way to such thoughts. Only one thing is needed: Are you willing to yield yourself up to God so that His Holy Spirit may get entire possession of you? This is surely what every Christian ought to seek. Review chapter twelve, "The Promise of the Father." Give time and heart to meditate on the wonderful mysteries: the Holy Spirit of God given to fill you with a divine life; the heavenly Father inconceivably willing to give the gift; the blessed Lord ready to teach you to pray and to lead you in the path that He took, through the death of the cross to the fullness of the Spirit; and your prayer, which can work the mighty wonder and bring the fullness of the Spirit.

Just follow the examples that Christ gives in Luke 11: a simple child trusting a father, a needy man persistently pleading with a friend. See if God will not pour out a blessing. Just remember that if you fail, you will be keeping open the path in which others fail, too. If you are strong and courageous, God will certainly use you to help others.

I know no other solution to the tremendous problem of lifting the church into a fuller spiritual life than this: Let each of us give himself for God to use. God is eager and able to do something for us that we have never yet known. Read Isaiah 6 until your awareness of your own powerlessness has been first deepened, then conquered, by the thought of the Holy God cleansing you with His fire. Oh, prepare yourself to say, "Here am I! Send me!"

As we have already seen:

There can be no forward movement in missions, no great offering of life, without a deepening of the spiritual life of the church leaders and a real spiritual revival among the church members ... The one real lack today is a lack of spiritual life; the one great need, the realization of the constant presence and power of the Holy Spirit.

It is this we need to pray for – a revival of true spiritual life – not, in the first place, a revival among the unconverted. God has given that in past years, but it is as if the mission outreaches do not have the access or hold that they had formerly.

It is as if God sees that the church is not living on the high spiritual level that equips her for bearing and rearing strong spiritual Christians. The converts come too much under the influence of a feeble spiritual life, and too many sink into worldliness and indifference.

We must plead with God for such a mighty renewal of the power of eternal life in His children's hearts that it will give them the intense devotion that marks a truly healthy soul. We need nothing less than the resurrection power of Jesus Christ.

I believe that there are three circles in every congregation: the large outer one of the scarcely saved; the small inner one of the truly devoted; and then the middle one of those who are always longing for a better life, and yet are so bound in their powerlessness that they know nothing of true victory.

Let us think especially of these and plead for

them that believers may be raised up, full of faith and the Holy Spirit, with the power to lead them to a clear vision of Christ. This will cause them to gladly and completely surrender to Him at once. And they will be assured of an all-sufficient strength for their lives in His service.

I plead with you to pray for missions, in all its different aspects, as never before. Yield yourself to the Holy Spirit for this work of intercession, and fervently ask God to bring the people in your congregation to such a life in Christ that it will make them a willing people in the day of His power. Set your heart on this. Give God no rest until His Spirit moves among His children in mighty power.

Cherish carefully the thought that you have yielded yourself to God to be set apart as an intercessor. He will work in you all the grace that is needed and give you the blessed assurance that you have power with Him. Live in the bold and holy confidence that God is ready to bless His church through you.

As this consciousness becomes stronger, you will be able to speak with others and testify, in the power of the Spirit, that God is really only waiting for prayer in order to give the blessing. Try to gather others who are of the same spirit for meetings and prayer.

Help each other to realize that you are definitely and persistently expecting God to lift His church into the abundant life. Cry day and night for it.

Help all to feel that this should first of all be the object of definite, secret prayer. Secret prayer will be the proof that your life has now been given up to the Holy Spirit. Let united prayer then be a witness to God and your own heart that you are sure that secret prayer will be answered.

If you are a minister, try to find other ministers who will give themselves to this great work in the spirit of entire self-sacrifice, confident faith, and persistent prayer. Help each of them to come to the full sense of his calling and the confident assurance that God will hear. Remember these words: "If some are resolutely and irrevocably led into the school of prayer, the spiritual power of the church for the accomplishment of its great task will be immeasurably increased." Believe that when you take part in such a ministry of prayer, it will be to you the beginning of a new life of blessing and strength.

Let me appeal to all of my readers, men and women, children of God. As you lay aside this book, do not refuse the pleading with which it closes, but tell God whether you now present yourself as a holy sacrifice to be at His disposal for the work of His Spirit. Let each of you say, "Here am I," until your whole being bows before

God in this living conviction: "God accepts me, God enables me, God will bless me. What He has never been able to do through me before, He can and will do now. I am His for the great work of helping to lift His church into the fuller life, which will overflow in blessing to a perishing world."

And let each one of us pray that every reader who has joined in the surrender may be blessed with a new discovery of what God will do through him.

Remember, everything depends in the first place on the individual yielding himself up.

Hints on Intercession

To be effective, intercession must be intelligent, definite, believing, and persevering. First of all, it must be intelligent. This means that we are not to be content with what others think or write. We must set ourselves with all our hearts to realize what it is that we are asking for. "Love the Lord your God with all your ... mind and with all your strength" (Mark 12:30). That applies to prayer, too.

Let us apply it to the great unsolved problem that has been occupying us and now calls for our prayers: How can the church be lifted up out of her low spiritual state into the abundant life that there is in Christ Jesus?

If one is really to pray effectively, he must prove to God that he feels grieved at the low spiritual condition of the church, and that he has set his heart on the blessing of the abundant life in Christ.

Just think for a moment of the proofs we have had of that feeble life:

- ✌ We have the verdict that the church as a whole is indifferent to the call to do the work for which she was placed in the world; therefore, she is spiritually unfit for taking part in it.
- ✌ We have the confession of the churches of their decline in membership. It is a proof that they are unable to drive back the spirit of the world.
- ✌ Both of these symptoms indicate a lack of spiritual life and power.
- ✌ With this there is the absolute impossibility of doing anything to bring about a change.

Take time and think through these points. Pray to God to give you a vision of their terrible reality, the grief and dishonor they are to Him, the terrible loss of souls that they imply, and the part that you have in it all.

Begin to admit what a great work it is that you are undertaking, to pray for that great revolution that is needed if a change is to come.

Pray for your ministers, pray for your congregation, pray for the believers with whom you have fellowship in prayer, pray for the whole church, that God may show us all what the true state of the church really is.

Unless we are willing to take time, to turn aside from the world to give ourselves to the holy exercise of laboring and striving in prayer, we have no right to hope for deliverance. It is a hard work, a difficult work, a solemn work. But let us not try to serve God with that which costs us nothing. It cost Christ everything, His blood and His life, to conquer death and win for us a share in His abundant life. If God's intercessors are to have power to prevail, they must learn in deep humility and contrition to truly give their whole lives and strength to bear the burden of the state of their fellow Christians.

Now, let us look on the other side, the abundant life that is waiting for the church, and see what basis there is for faith and hope in prayer.

What is impossible with men is possible with God. God has given to His church the promise of the Holy Spirit, who has the divine power that will equip her for the work she has to do.

The more we carefully study the state of the church – the worldly life of the majority of her members, the tremendous difficulty of rousing even a single congregation to a higher spiritual life, the lack of power in her ministers, even many who long for better times – the more deeply we will feel the hopelessness of having a true revival, one in which Christians will really yield themselves wholly to a new life in Christ Jesus. But let this impossibility be just what drives us into the arms of God and into a new faith in what He can do.

Think of how Christ has promised that the Father will give the gift of the Holy Spirit to those who request it. Think of that until your whole heart is filled with the assurance that God can, and will, must (we say it reverently) give His Spirit where His believing people unite in whole-hearted prayer and consecration.

With this, think of the very special power that has been given to prayer, and the boundless possibilities to which it gives us the key. Take time – if you want to exercise yourself in prayer and learn the art of intercession – to let all the promises of answers to prayer fill you with the confident assurance of what is going to come. This is one of the great privileges of prayer: it throws you upon God and opens your heart so that He may make His promises a personal gift to you.

Begin then, and take time. Just as you have examined the state of the church in its feebleness and sin, begin to study God's Word as if, for the first time, you were trying to find out what God has really promised to do for His church here on earth.

Take Christ's teaching in John 14-16, and believe that the power of the Holy Spirit is meant to make the following promise a reality: "If anyone loves Me ... My Father will love him, and we will come to him and make our home with him" (John 14:23).

Take the experience of Paul, in all that Christ did for him, and regard that as a pattern of what God is willing to do now. Steadfastly ask God to definitely work in you, in those around you, and in His church in its low state, what He has promised. Do not rest until the vision of what God is willing to do fills your heart so that you can think of nothing else. You have given your whole life to be occupied with this as its chief aim; do not rest until your heart is fully possessed with it.

Then you will be prepared to take your place as an intercessor in power. Your prayers will become more intelligent, but also more fervent, more believing and more persevering.

You will begin to understand something of what prayer means in its fullness – a taking hold of God, a giving Him no rest, a going on to be persistent in prayer until faith receives the quiet assurance that God will give what is asked.

Pray, above all, for the gift of the Holy Spirit to

have entire possession of both you and all God's children who are pleading for the new life. Pray fervently, determinedly, for the ministers who are willing to yield themselves to God's work. Pray for all ministers as the leaders of the flock of God. Give yourself as a whole sacrifice to God for the great work of seeking the revival of His church and, through her, the evangelization of the world.

God seeks intercessors. God has need of intercessors. God is concerned about the lack of intercessors. Do not rest until God sees that you are one.

You are called ...
To pray for missions as never before and be confident that God is ready to bless His church through you.

Other books by
Andrew Murray

Humility is the only ladder to the highest honor in God's kingdom. In this precious book Andrew Murray puts an entirely new light on this little understood Christian grace and shows that humble dependence on God is the basis of all genuine blessing.

ISBN 1-86852-940-1

In *Absolute Surrender* Andrew Murray states that there is no other choice for us; we must either deny self or Christ. If I am something, then God is not everything; but when I become nothing, God can become all.

ISBN 1-86920-112-4

Discover the secrets of enjoying God's presence, becoming one with other believers, preparing for spiritual warfare, and obeying the heavenly Father. *Living to Please God* will guide readers into a fruitful life as a bondservant of Jesus Christ as they learn to please Him in everything they do.

ISBN 1-86920-427-1

In *The Deeper Christian Life* Andrew Murray shows readers the importance of taking time to meet God and yielding their whole lives to Him. Murray prompts readers to turn from being self-willed, self-pleasing and self-sufficient into total dependence on God so they can live a life of abundance.

ISBN 1-86920-130-2

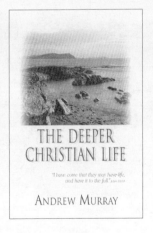